More than a "rock bio," Michelle Leon has writt[e]
iness of self-realization, and the provisional sal[
love. It's also about being in an important all-g
time, documenting a scene that still resonates. It's profound, poetic,
tender, and inspiring. You know someone who needs this, and they might
just be you.

—WILL HERMES, AUTHOR OF *LOVE GOES TO BUILDINGS ON FIRE: FIVE YEARS IN NEW YORK CITY THAT CHANGED MUSIC FOREVER*

Michelle Leon has provided us with a crucial and compelling account of what it was to be a woman making music in the nineties. Leon was the first woman on stage that I wanted to be. I have been waiting for this book for twenty years. Fantastic and ferocious.

—JESSICA HOPPER, MUSIC AND CULTURE CRITIC AND AUTHOR OF *THE FIRST COLLECTION OF CRITICISM BY A LIVING FEMALE ROCK CRITIC* AND *THE GIRLS' GUIDE TO ROCKING*

Babes in Toyland may have showed Riot Grrrl how to scream, but their dirty, roiling noise called to hips and heart as much as fists. Likewise, former BiT bassist Michelle Leon's haunting memoir is more than the story of a girl in a band. This visceral and thoughtful *On the Road* illustrates a continuing quandary of contemporary life: Is there a way to forge identity beyond what you choose to consume? And what happens when alternatives to the mainstream prove equally unwilling to acknowledge your tender peculiarities, your spidery contradictions, your griefs both ancient and newborn?

—TERRI SUTTON, FREELANCE WRITER AND FORMER *CITY PAGES* ARTS EDITOR

I've seldom heard anyone capture the surreality of fleeting rock and roll fame as well as Michelle Leon—I once heard her describe going in 24 hours from cheering English fans at Heathrow to mopping a floor in her south Minneapolis apartment. In her book she juggles the historically significant and the prosaic with equal aplomb and sensitivity. The sensory veil of Bonnie Bell lip gloss, velvet wallpaper, fingers sliding on a bass, syringes in wastebaskets envelops you. No punches are pulled, yet no band members are eviscerated—their humanity revealed. True to the humble Minneapolis narrative spirit, there is little or no name-dropping for its own sake. While Michelle tells the story with a wide-eyed wonder and naïveté of one first initiated to the vortex of Minneapolis music, you never lose track of the significance and place of her band in the big picture. She'd never say it but: Where would Pussy Riot be without Babes in Toyland?

—ADAM LEVY, SINGER-SONGWRITER (THE HONEYDOGS)

Maybe you know the words to every Babes in Toyland song; maybe you've never heard the band's music at all. No matter: by the end of this lyrical, tough, and moving memoir, you'll not only feel like you know Michelle Leon, you'll also want to talk and dance and listen to music with her. Most of all, you'll want to recommend this book to anyone who's ever wondered what it's like to be a woman in the strange, sometimes brutal world of contemporary American rock and roll.

—SCOTT HEIM, AUTHOR OF *MYSTERIOUS SKIN* AND *WE DISAPPEAR*

I Live Inside feels as real and personal as reading your own memories. Michelle tells the bittersweet story of Babes in Toyland's nonstop touring/recording schedule and all the grime, laughs, jealousy, love, pain, horror, and glory that came with it. Parts read like a fairy tale while others are so haunting they will never leave you.

—KELLI MAYO, MUSICIAN (SKATING POLLY)

I wanted to buy a copy of this book for all my friends and family as soon as I finished reading it. Babes in Toyland's work ethic is beyond inspiring, and Michelle's fear of not being quite good enough is all too relatable. You'll feel like a fly on the wall as Babes navigate through the underground rock scene.

—PEYTON BIGHORSE, MUSICIAN (SKATING POLLY)

Michelle Leon's story of indie rock stardom is both raw and readable. I love this book for its close, intimate details. Leon draws you right into the Babes in Toyland van and shows you the after party tensions and what is in the mind of this particular girl in a band.

—DARCEY STEINKE, AUTHOR OF *SISTER GOLDEN HAIR: A NOVEL* AND OTHERS

Beautiful, sad and happy, poignant yet humble. The prose is lyrical and witty, and Michelle refreshingly nails the truth of the "shit happens" loop of life as a touring musician in a van, mixed with moving yet always unassuming explorations into love and loss and the human psyche. I never had too many chances to see Babes in Toyland—I too was living in a parallel yet not entirely different version of "my own inside"—but when I did, they scared the hell out of me, which I can only assume was the point.

—DANIEL D. MURPHY, MUSICIAN, SONGWRITER, AND GUITARIST (SOUL ASYLUM, GOLDEN SMOG)

I Live Inside is Michelle Leon's thrilling, riveting, and sometimes heartrending account of her years as the bassist for the seminal indie rock band Babes in Toyland. Her prose is stunning, her eye is wry, and her heart enormous; the result is a compelling memoir filled with pop culture, travel, intrigue, and a young artist's quest to find her voice. *I Live Inside* is loud and clear, and I could not put it down.

—LAURIE LINDEEN, MUSICIAN (ZUZU'S PETALS) AND AUTHOR OF
PETAL PUSHER: A ROCK AND ROLL CINDERELLA STORY

If Orpheus played bass, Virgil wore lingerie, and Persephone ever told people how she really felt. . . . This masterful, gentle soul is the perfect guide through the sensual, destructive, rich, and violent times in the underground rock scene of the 1980s and '90s. Unique and poetic, Michelle's prose is a voice, rhythmic, resonant, and our conduit to a forbidden world. We knew her, were her, but we never did this.

—KEVIN KLING, AUTHOR, PLAYWRIGHT, AND STORYTELLER

Tough chicks tenderly portrayed, one girl's view into the bubbling energy of the Minneapolis rock scene—filled with vivid, personal detail, evocative lists, and reflections on a time that still feels raw. The form is clipped and episodic, propelling the reader through the alternating kaleidoscopes of boredom and self-inflicted chaos that typify a life in music. Michelle feels and tells the story as one who was at the center of the swirling energy that characterized a unique moment in music.

—JOHN MUNSON, MUSICIAN AND BASS PLAYER (TRIP SHAKESPEARE,
SEMISONIC, THE TWILIGHT HOURS, THE NEW STANDARDS)

Michelle Leon writes with rare insight and sensitivity not about a life in rock and roll but of the rock and roll in her life and how one nourished and informed the other. She describes as no other music memoir the struggles and transcendence that playing in a band brings: The love and impatience she feels for her bandmates and they for her; how to find her true identity within the band and completely outside of it; the forced intimacy and alienation of life on the road; the sacrifices and rewards that rock and roll demands and provides the perceptive introvert alone on a stage yet wholly engaged with the music and her audience. A singular, insightful, brave tale of an artist coming to terms with her art and herself.

—DAVID N. MEYER, AUTHOR OF *TWENTY THOUSAND ROADS:
THE BALLAD OF GRAM PARSONS AND HIS COSMIC AMERICAN MUSIC*

In finely drawn vignettes, Michelle Leon's memoir *I Live Inside* captures not only the exhilaration of performing but also the quiet loneliness found off-stage. A vivid tale of rock and roll's thrills and secret heartbreaks awaits you on the pages of this haunting book.

—JACOB SLICHTER, MUSICIAN, DRUMMER (SEMISONIC),
AND AUTHOR OF *SO YOU WANNA BE A ROCK & ROLL STAR*

It is always exciting to have another side to a story, and here is Michelle's, touring through the time when she played—first with lent bass, in the desire to join, along with Lori, "badass, a punk cave girl, tattooed and dressed in black," Kat's notes going "pink to red as the words travel from a place that is primal, formed to communicate some kind of pain." Complicated, consoling, and true in all the enchantments of dress, the candid colors, songs, and background in girl loving music and that lost Joe Cole.

—DOUGLAS A. MARTIN, AUTHOR OF *ONCE YOU GO BACK*

"What's it like to be a girl in a band?" Ugh. Next question! Michelle Leon's *I Live Inside* tells what it's like to be a *person* in a band. And then—suddenly, painfully—a person who used to be in a band. A vivid, poetic memoir.

—MARK YARM, AUTHOR OF *EVERYBODY LOVES OUR TOWN:
AN ORAL HISTORY OF GRUNGE*

Michelle Leon's intimate, heartfelt, and heart-aching portrait of an emerging Minneapolis female (punk) rocker. Real names'd be proof. This is Planet Leon.

—DAVID MARKEY, FILMMAKER, AUTHOR, AND MUSICIAN

I LIVE INSIDE

MEMOIRS OF A BABE IN TOYLAND

MICHELLE LEON

MINNESOTA
HISTORICAL
SOCIETY PRESS

Song lyrics credits and photo credits are included at the back of the book.

www.mnhspress.org
The Minnesota Historical Society Press is a member of the Association of American University Presses.

Manufactured in the United States of America

10 9 8 7 6 5 4 3 2 1

∞ The paper used in this publication meets the minimum requirements of the American National Standard for Information Sciences—Permanence for Printed Library Materials, ANSI Z39.48-1984.

Cover photo by Brian Garrity

ISBN: 978-0-87351-998-4 (cloth)
ISBN: 978-0-87351-999-1 (e-book)

LIBRARY OF CONGRESS CATALOGING-IN-PUBLICATION DATA
Names: Leon, Michelle, 1969– author.
Title: I live inside : memoirs of a babe in toyland / Michelle Leon.
Description: Saint Paul, MN : Minnesota Historical Society, 2016.
Identifiers: LCCN 2015037028 | ISBN 9780873519984 (cloth : alk. paper) |
    ISBN 9780873519991 (ebook)
Subjects: LCSH: Leon, Michelle, 1969– | Babes in Toyland (Musical group) |
    Guitarists—United States—Biography. | Women rock musicians—United
    States—Biography.
Classification: LCC ML419.L427 L46 2016 | DDC 782.42166092/2—dc23
LC record available at http://lccn.loc.gov/2015037028

This and other Minnesota Historical Society Press books are available from popular e-book vendors.

To Joe

FEBRUARY 17, 2015

My son is squirming and wiggling, descending, almost ready to arrive. Today is his due date. I have a perfect reason to be sitting at Nina's coffee shop in St. Paul finishing the manuscript I began writing in 2009, trying to wrap it up before he gets here.

This is the prologue I didn't expect to write, the same way I never expected to be a first-time mother in my forties. When I take breaks and look at the Internet, it is filled with stories about Babes in Toyland's reunion shows, the first since 2001.

I never pictured this reunion taking place. I feel a mixture of pride, wistfulness, and—as much as I hate to admit it—a little like the kid left out on the playground. I'm not the girl in the pictures with Lori and Kat. And I realize this is the perfect beginning and ending to this story, the way it continues, still surprising and affecting me, still meaningful and a trigger to a whole range of emotions.

I am so excited for my friends to be making music together again.

I miss those days so much.

I can't believe that I will soon hold my son.

I am so happy that you are about to read *my* story.

This is how I remember it. Some names and places have been changed.

THINGS I'VE BEEN TOLD

You are not the prettiest girl in the room. You look really horny when you play. Your butt is too big to be a bass player. His blood stained the sidewalk. She stopped breathing, turned blue, then came back. I might have given you crabs. You're always mumbling. When you were leaning over, I could see your boobs. You wouldn't make a good mother. Someone broke into the van and stole your guitar.

WHAT MY MOTHER TOLD ME

"I never was able to think of you as this little helpless baby because you never were. You wouldn't sit in an infant seat; as soon as I'd put you in, you'd start squirming and yelling, trying to crawl out. It was obvious even before you were born—you were always kicking and moving around—you just had that kind of temperament, the need to see the world and experience things."

With my mom on a Leon family trip to Pennsylvania Dutch country, 1971

THEY'RE WAITING FOR US

As we leave Minneapolis, the houses become tiny, looking down from above. The cars move like toys. The three of us seated together on the plane, snuggled in blankets and pillows, eye masks and stocking feet, heads resting on each other's shoulders. Little bottles of wine. It's June 10, 1991. We're on our way to London for the *To Mother* tour; we heard our record's doing well there. A month of shows scheduled in the U.K., the Netherlands, Germany, and France, all the way to Yugoslavia, and finally ending with the Reading Festival, a huge outdoor music festival back in England.

Some mornings I wake up and don't know where I am, what language people are speaking, what the currency is worth. Old ladies ask me questions I can't understand. I smile idiotically in return.

Pointing at my choice of delicious pastry in the bakery display, paying the counter girl by holding my money as if showing a hand of cards, letting her pick. Going into a drugstore, my sore feet in some new foxy European shoes, showing the pharmacist my blisters and frowning; my way of asking where the Band-Aids are.

Ancient buildings tower in the sky. Each of us with our own room in the lovely hotels, beds with extra-soft quilts. Sitting on benches and watching people walk by.

In Paris, we go to the Père Lachaise Cemetery, where Jim Morrison and Edith Piaf and Oscar Wilde are buried.

BABES IN TOYLAND

JUNE	13	LONDON Mean Fiddler
	14	LIVERPOOL Planet X
	15	LEEDS Duchess of York
	16	BIRMINGHAM Edward's No 8
	17	NEWCASTLE Riverside
	19	UTRECHT Tivoli
	20	NIJMEGEN Doornroosje
	21	ROTTERDAM De Vlerk
	22	DEVENTER Burgerweeshuis
	23	EINDHOVEN De Effenaar
	25	ZAGREB
	26	BELGRADE
	28	DORNBIRN Spielboden
	29	EBENSEE Festival
	30	MUNICH Nachtwerk

To Mother

JULY	01	KOLN Rose Club
	02	HAMBURG Fabrik
	04	BERLIN Loft
	05	MUNSTER Odeon
	06	DORTMUND FSW
	08	KARLSRUHE Katakombe
	09	PARIS Gibus Club
	11	GRONINGEN Vera
	12	AMSTERDAM Paradiso
	13	FONTENAY LE COMTE Festival
	14	GENT Democrazy
	15	LONDON ULU
AUG	23	READING Festival

European tour, 1991

Wandering around in a light rain. The aboveground tombs with ornately carved cherubs and crosses, the dead flowers left graveside by mourners.

The morning we first arrive in London, John Loder from our record label takes us to our first stop, an in-store appearance at a record shop. He tells us *To Mother* is #1 on the indie charts. We whiz past double-decker buses and billboards advertising biscuits, pulling up to the Virgin Megastore on Oxford Street. People are lined up around the block.

They're waiting for us.

We get out of the car and photographers are yelling our names, the sound of cameras snapping, flashbulbs, shouting like little birds. We are very tired and can only look at each other and laugh. Each time someone calls out one of our names, we laugh even harder.

I PICTURE MYSELF INSIDE

I first see Babes in Toyland play at a party in Minneapolis. I'm seventeen years old. The band is a four-piece, all girls. A lead singer named Cindy with long black hair and a hint of stoner-witch spinning around holding flowing scarves that trail behind her like wings. A willowy bass player, Chris, Cindy's best friend, so lovely and proficient.

Lori, the drummer, pounding with the butt-end of her sticks, hammering the kick drum with her bare feet. HARD, badass, a punk cave girl, tattooed and dressed in black.

A sandy-blonde guitar player named Kat sings one of the songs. The screams she lets out are abrasive; I imagine her throat turning from pink to red as the words travel from a place that is primal, formed to communicate some kind of pain. She is Carroll Baker lying in the crib in *Baby Doll*, she is punk rock, California beach, and straitjacket; she is a purple thistle blooming in the patch of stinging nettles. She is perfect. Someone I imagine living moments more dreamy and seedy than I could ever know.

As I watch them play their set, the thoughts flash in my mind: walking down railroad tracks drinking gin from a mason jar; playing guitar and hanging out all night long; beautiful long-haired boys with baby faces and hairless chests all wanting to make out with me; gold confetti falling from the sky. I picture myself in the middle. I picture myself inside. Somehow I know this will come true.

A friend lends me a $75 Sears sunburst bass. I buy a book at Schmitt Music showing all the notes. I teach myself how to play.

BEER AND LOVE'S BABY SOFT

Your parents always say you live in Minnetonka, one of the fancier suburbs of Minneapolis. Your house is in Minnetonka, but the backyard is in Hopkins, where you say you live. Hopkins, "The Raspberry Capital of the World," with little old houses, a main street with dive bars, a trailer park. The gardens of Minnetonka landscaped with expertly trimmed bushes and big dull rocks, often owned by fancy ladies with long nails and tiny dogs—you know those aren't real gardens. Not like the ones in Hopkins, decorated with milk cans, overgrown with wild flowers, old ladies in housecoats pulling weeds along the walkways leading to the back.

On Hobby Oak Drive, your house has a very special kind of 1970s swankiness. Built by the previous owner, the former mayor of Hopkins, the place is lush with velvet-textured wallpaper, scrolling black ironwork railings, a different color of shag carpet in each bedroom, and a bar in the basement made of puffy black vinyl and gold buttons.

You're eleven years old. Your parents go out of town overnight and leave your sixteen-year-old brother in charge. Your even-older sister moved out three years ago. That night, you get confined to your parents' bedroom with a bag of Cheetos, an assortment from the Pop Shoppe, and a small black-and-white TV. A garbage can with a keg on ice sits next to the garden tools and snow shovels in the garage.

In your parents' room, a wall of mirrors opens into a huge closet with a secret changing room in back. You hang out in there trying on your mom's nighties, her cocktail dresses and jewelry. You are especially into her enormous "War Is Not Healthy for Children and Other Living Things" pendant and the one with the googly-eyed owl.

Later, you get bored and sneak downstairs in your pj's to see what's going on. It's super loud. The Who's *Tommy*, Santana, and KQ92, classic rock live from Dibbo's in Hudson, Wisconsin, what you imagine to be the coolest bar on earth. Snow boots piled on the straw welcome mat and teenage boys in your living room, sitting on the couch where you watch *The Wide World of Disney* and Saturday-morning cartoons.

In the kitchen, guys make drinks in your mom's blender. The teenage girls coming in the door are so foxy with their fur-hooded parkas with lift tickets on the zippers, hair expertly curled, lips shining with strawberry roll-on gloss. You run back upstairs.

Some of those girls later discover you in your parents' room. They are acting so weird: stumbling, being too nice, talking loud, smelling like beer and Love's Baby Soft. You don't care. They're curling your hair. You watch *Fantasy Island* together.

In the morning, you go downstairs and see a hole in the hallway from a drunken fight. Your pink bathroom rug is wadded up in the corner of the kitchen. Both boys and girls sleeping on the floor of your family room, only messy hair showing out the tops of their sleeping bags. You swear to your brother that you won't tell.

Your parents come home on Sunday night and find out

anyway: that hole, and a neighbor lady called. There is lots of yelling. You hear your brother cry. You stay in your bedroom and turn your clock radio to KQ92, singing along to Heart's "Magic Man," your door shut tight.

YOUR GRANDMA'S CLOTHES

In high school, I carry a notebook full of my writing. Spiders, death, and darkness are the most common themes. The poetry page in the back of *Rolling Stone* magazine, my favorite part. Black eye pencil always sketched onto the delicate pink of my lower rim, outfits from Ragstock, a giant used-clothing warehouse in Minneapolis, spending hours digging though gigantic musty barrels to find the vintage dresses and sweaters.

"Are those your grandma's clothes?" the girls in the bathroom at Hopkins High cackle.

Taking the 17C bus to downtown Minneapolis, I shop at Northern Lights Music on Block E, a stretch of Hennepin Avenue with strip clubs, dive bars, and Rifle Sport, the underground art gallery that puts on punk rock shows, which are still a little too scary for me. At Northern Lights, I buy cassettes of Aztec Camera, Spandau Ballet, David Bowie, Elvis Costello, and The Fall. I spend hours in the two-story shop, looking through everything, absorbing it all.

Next door at First Avenue and 7th Street Entry, I go to as many all-ages shows as I can. Smoking clove cigarettes and talking to boys way older than me; they call a few days later. The humiliation of my mom answering the phone and yelling my name, those uncomfortable conversations, my wicked shyness. Sitting on the steps leading to our basement, twirling the spiral phone cord around my wrist. A short, skinny Jewish girl with giant eyes and dark curly hair.

"Did you play sports when you were in school?" I ask, the best I have for conversation.

They never call again.

GIRL CRUSHES

My girl crushes are almost always in bands, whether the main attraction, the backup singer, or the tambourine player. Laurie Partridge, all big-eyed and bell-sleeved, rocking the keyboard; Janis Joplin howling with her wild hair; Patti Smith's armpit hair, rough-feathery voice and lyrics ("Dancing Barefoot," the sexiest song ever—oh man, that rant at the end); Stevie Nicks's '70s hippie-on-the-beach look in scarves, chokers, and lace; even Gilda Radner as Candy Slice—braless, alcohol-soaked, and falling down—stirred something in me as I watched *Saturday Night Live* after my bedtime as a ten-year-old.

Seeing Babes in Toyland play the first time at that party in Minneapolis, I knew that was it, it was *everything*: the exact kind of woman I wanted to be, or maybe almost was.

Women musicians are extraordinary, mysterious, powerful, and compelling. Each time one of these celestial beings comes into my orbit, it is stunning and exciting. Being a rock guy is just cliché.

MY MOM TAKES ME TO TARGET

I get a fake ID, leave high school, and take courses at the University of Minnesota in the post-secondary program instead. Writing papers about Flannery O'Connor and Tennessee Williams. No prom, no ceremony, just eventually enough credits to graduate high school, my diploma arriving in the mail. I move out of my parents' house and into an apartment above the most choice old-guy bar/music scene bar in town, the CC Club.

My dad is a cardiologist. Mom is a psychologist who sued Rutgers University in 1973 for sex discrimination when they refused to promote her. She won, giving part of her settlement to NOW. Both say I'm too young to go, but little by little my things disappear in the used Ford Escort they bought me and end up at that place. I begin to stay every night. My roommate is a crabby punk rock girl named Jennifer, introduced by a mutual friend. Sheets for curtains, yellow foam from Jo-Ann Fabric with a blanket on top as my bed, pictures of bands cut out of magazines and taped to the walls, brown water spots on the ceiling, stained carpet, peeling paint, clogged toilet, the sound of the jukebox and customers downstairs. My mom takes me to Target and buys me a napkin holder, paper towels, and cleaning supplies. I am so embarrassed to be seen with her. The squalor of my new home brings constant disquiet to her mind.

On steamy summer days, I walk across the street to Oar Folkjokeopus record store and comb through the racks. I look at the posters covering the walls, all my favorite local bands—Blue Hippos, Urban Guerillas, Hüsker Dü—and touring bands I'm discovering, like Camper Van Beethoven and Violent Femmes. The clerks make me nervous. Oar Folk feels small and intimidating, lacking the invisibility of Northern Lights. I'm so afraid of not being cool. I don't know what records to pick, so I don't buy anything except the latest issue of *Trouser Press* magazine.

Sitting on my window ledge, knees tucked into my chest, sundress and bare feet, looking out over Lyndale Avenue. Cars drive by and people talk on the sidewalk; Jennifer sleeps in the next room without the privacy of a door.

SO SMALL

During happy hour at Lyle's, the bar where I work, I dump giant buckets of chicken wings into the warming tray of the buffet, next to the plastic container of pickled herring and a giant block of cheese the other waitresses and I call "The Cheese Lick." Later we pick up the paper plates scattered around the bar soaked through with greasy wing remains. "Bone Patrol." The owners never ask my age.

I get a cherry blossom branch tattoo on my left thigh as soon as I turn eighteen and go to rock shows every night possible, either with my roommate or alone. The darkness and the noise, the swirling sexual energy, the crowds and sweat all relieve my spinning brain. Dancing until I have blisters to the snaky groove of Run Westy Run, or the sweet soulfulness of the Jayhawks, the jumping-up-and-down rock of Soul Asylum, or the insane noise of Cows. I try to make friends with girls who are more confident and older than I am.

I like working and making my own money, carrying trays full of beer and wiping tables with a towel. I keep my dollar bills organized and am slick handing back change. I like living in a crappy apartment above a bar. I like boys. Even when I don't have anything to say, they still listen to me.

I meet Grant at a party, messy head of shoulder-length curls, Levi's ripped at the knees, Hüsker Dü t-shirt. He is persistent, wanting to make out, but he is also easy to ignore. When I realize he is the drummer for Soul Asylum, I am much nicer. I recognize my shallowness. Still, when Grant rolls up on his skateboard late at night and throws rocks at my window, I let him in.

We hang out downstairs at the CC Club. I stand quietly to the side while Grant talks to everyone, though he always introduces me. The sound of my own voice makes me panic, prickly and hot, a constant blush on my face and chest. I soon learn the way alcohol eases my shyness, especially tequila sunrises.

We play pool. I'm a lousy shot, but keep trying. One late afternoon, my ball flies off the table and rolls across the floor, the clatter resonating throughout the room. I hear a booming laugh and look across the room; this woman is pointing at me and howling in hysterics, happy like a cartoon bear.

Grant introduces me to his friend Lori Barbero, famous for her magic mushroom "tea parties," I'm told. She's been part of the scene for as long as he can remember. I am too nervous to tell her that I saw her band play at that warehouse party; I'll have Grant mention later how much I loved them. With her long, bleached-blonde hair and red lips, her beautiful face shining, reflecting her half-Filipino, half-Scandinavian descent. She is three-quarters punk rock, one-quarter pin-up. And she is talking to me, telling me to sit next to her. More drinks and talking dirty about flying balls. She tells me bad jokes:

"Do you know that beer makes you smart?"

"No, why?"

"It made Budweiser."

Her attention makes me feel not quite so small.

NO MISTAKES

"Smoke on the Water," "Cocaine," and the bass solo to Fleetwood Mac's "The Chain," that's all I know. But when I hear that Babes in Toyland's singer and bass player both left the band, I tap into my bravest self. That night, I go to First Avenue to look for Lori.

I find out that Kat's been in bands for years in Portland and San Francisco, including Sugar Babydoll with her friends Courtney Love and Jennifer Finch. At twenty-four, Kat moved to Minneapolis for the music scene and met Lori at a barbecue. Lori had just bought her first kit from the drummer of Run Westy Run and, at the age of twenty-five, was teaching herself how to play.

"What are you doing?" Lori asks when I finally spot her at the club.

"I really want to talk to you," I say.

"What do you want to do?"

Grant has already discussed it with her, and it seems decided. Even though I haven't met Kat yet, with the exception of serving her a few drinks at Lyle's, Lori gives me the address and we schedule our first practice. Sometimes the extraordinary is so ordinary.

I can't decide what to wear and go with the "tough girl" look—jeans, engineer boots, '70s lace shirt—when I meet Lori and Kat at their practice space in the basement of the "Big Trouble House," the Victorian duplex where Lori lives.

On stage, 1989

After Cindy and Chris left the group, Lori and Kat decided to become a three-piece, like Minutemen, one of Lori's favorite bands, with Kat singing lead and playing guitar.

Kat teaches me a song. She points to my guitar to show me the notes because it's easier than remembering what they are called. I play with my fingers instead of a pick, even though it hurts, because I'm told that's how "real" bass players are supposed to play.

"Hit this string open. Then press this dot. Then open again. Then this one."

And that is pretty much all you need to know to play bass in Babes in Toyland.

Kat sings the words written in her notebook.

Grandma's girl is coming down
To steal violets from
your crown,
Glue them to her wrist.
You have to spit to see the shine

I played "Spit to See the Shine" all the way through. No mistakes.

HOG PILE

They kick me out of the band when Courtney Love moves to Minneapolis and wants to be their bass player. They practice one or two times. Lori calls a week later, while I'm working lunch at Lyle's. She asks me to come back.

I say OK, but I have to go refill the chili-mac and saltines at the soup bar.

And now they are both being extra nice to me

We consider changing the name of the band to Swamp Pussy, to make it a fresh start, but that idea ultimately gets turned down.

"No way am I saying the words *swamp pussy* to my parents," I tell them, kidding. But I also mean it.

Our first show is in the basement of an art gallery. We carry our equipment down the steps and set up. There is no stage, only our stuff on the floor in the corner, the three of us packed together tightly in the dark, mildewy space. The small crowd, mostly our friends, stand right next to us. Lori is not sure which drums to play when the soundman asks her to hit the high-hat and snare.

My hands shake as I plug the vintage blonde Fender P-Bass I bought with my tips into my borrowed amp. I am terrified and can only stand completely still as we perform, chewing my lips, turning bright red, concentrating so hard on hitting the right notes and mostly succeeding. I can barely hear Lori or Kat, only my loud bass clanging.

Lori flipping up her eyelids and freaking me out, 1989

Kat's screaming makes people uncomfortable. Lori keeps missing beats. I am totally stiff, frightened, focused, hyper-aware of everyone staring as I struggle. We are so relieved when we finally make it through our half-hour set. Some of the crowd felt sorry for us, I later learn, yet others felt something rare taking place.

After the show, we drink a few beers, a few swigs from somebody's flask, big hugs from our friends. Then Lori yells "hog-pile!" and the three of us drunk-wrestle on the dirty floor, blazing, ecstatic.

LORI'S INTERVIEW

I am so psyched reading this local fanzine that prints the first story about us, an interview with Lori. I skim through the story, scoping the text for my name. And there it is: Lori says that she and Kat couldn't rename the band Swamp Pussy like they wanted to because Michelle was too worried about what her parents would think.

I feel like I'm going to be sick. She thinks *I'm* a pussy. She does not mind telling this to all of Minneapolis

SCANTIES

Twinkle lights glow through old gauzy curtains with tea-colored stains, blurring the world outside and shining through bottles of ruby red wine. We work on new songs, playing through little practice amps, sitting on the bed. Papers scratched with lyrics are everywhere, mixed with the sheets and pillows, the peach-colored comforter, both satiny and quilted, the headboard made of wrought iron shaped into flowers and painted white.

A Victrola in the corner spins around a forgotten, scratchy old recording, a sad lady singing about being let down and left all alone. Candles burning and radiating, simple fat pillars melting in a teacup saucer and Mexican prayer candles; the Virgin de Guadalupe staring downward, hands folded in prayer, light shining from the center of her heart.

This is the first time I've been to Kat's apartment. This velvet girl-world is so stealth, like when my older cousins let me stay in the room while they smoked pot and listened to Led Zeppelin. She lets me try on her French perfume, Fracas, scented with tuberose and musk, and read her journals written in swirly script. I want her to stop talking while I read every single word.

Vintage lingerie all over the floor: white slip, black garter, pink crepe chemise with fabric rose, ruffled bloomers open at the crotch. She calls these pieces her scanties. Everything in her place is soft like a Valentine's Day candy

Kat at the old Loring Bar

box. A black-and-white picture tucked into the trim of her '30s dressing table—Kat, a toddler, withdrawn and lonely, the dewy curls make me want to smell her young head.

In the bathroom, the sight of syringes and cotton balls in the garbage can—not covered or pushed to the bottom—medical, dotted with residual blood. Bruises on her arms the color of eggplant at the holes where the needles enter and the opiate starts to travel through her system, tunneling though the chambers and vesicles of her heart, alive and breathing, arriving at the center of her brain and leaving her completely erased.

THINKING ABOUT CRICKETS

You go on a hayride at the orchard, horses tromping through the woods as you rest against a bale. Returning with cider and apples as golden leaves glide down from the sky and blow across the road during the drive home.

Your dad brings you out into the country to the Renaissance Festival. You eat a turkey drumstick that is way too big for you to finish while watching actors portray the days of yore, when everything was soaked in velvet and mead. Your dad buys you a feather on a clip to wear in your hair, neither of you realizing it's for smoking joints.

Your mom takes you shopping at Knollwood Mall for back-to-school clothes, third grade, the trunk of the car later filled with bags and boxes from Donaldson's, Kinney's Shoes, and the County Seat, where you get three colors of Levi's cords: forest green, sky blue, and rust. Notebooks and new pencils, pink erasers you are dying to chew. A lunch-box with Scooby Doo on the front, a matching thermos; you want to be just like Daphne and not at all like Velma.

Laying out the outfit you plan to wear the first day of school the night before; those cords, those shoes. Not being able to sleep, thinking about fuzzy sheep jumping over fences, thinking about crickets rubbing their back legs together like they're playing violin. They are all awake, just like you.

LEAVES

Our songs form like autumn in reverse, starting with bare branches. Leaves of gold, wine, and flame rise from the ground and find their place on the limbs. Eventually turning green, full blooms, feeding from the earth, feeding from our hearts.

Kat usually brings a song structure to practice, the foundation. I find notes that match or melodies to complement the chords. Sometimes Lori starts with a heavy drumbeat, the rhythm powerful, simple, complete. I know what to do. The songs rise from dormancy, assembling in layers.

In the basement of Big Trouble House, our equipment is set up around a giant octopus furnace near the gas meter and electrical box, pipes running overhead. Our practice space is big enough that actual shows are performed here, mostly the impromptu after-bar kind.

As we rehearse, Lori's roommates can only hear part of what we play—thundering bass and drums, Kat's roar. They usually leave the house.

One day a blackbird creeps in the window and flies around as we practice. The bird is dead when we finish, lying on its side, eyes open, beak shut.

Between songs, Lori complains: she's been working a lot; a boy is ignoring her; that girl thinks she's little and precious; someone owes her money. It's all recorded on cassette tapes marked BABES IN TOYLAND in Lori's florid handwriting. We use a giant boombox; one of us simultaneously hits play and record before starting a song. The recordings sometimes shut off with the sound of footsteps shuffling toward the tape deck, the loud click of one of us hitting the stop button.

The washer and dryer are also in this space. Sometimes Lori's roommates do their laundry while we're practicing. One of them tells us about a hole he noticed in the ceiling by the dryer. Looking closer, he saw something in the opening. He reached in and pulled out a small turn-of-the-century wooden soldier. This must have been a child's secret hiding place decades ago. Using a coat hanger, he dug further, pulling out more toys: porcelain dolls with arms and legs missing, a metal car, a bell, lead knights and horses, a broken wheel, a wooden top.

That muggy space in the summertime; cobwebs, stray socks, dryer lint, beer bottles, guitar cases, lyrics on a music stand. The freedom. A new definition of home.

ALPHA

I always feel like part of the chorus, a singer in a white Greek robe, everything about me just blending in. My family had a live-in housekeeper and season tickets to the ballet. These facts make me feel insubstantial, especially in the music scene, but also in general.

Kat looks like Brigitte Bardot after a hundred hits of acid: petite, C cup, just-fucked hair, composed even when she is coming apart. The drugs not so much shocking as they are fascinating. At this point, she hides the worst moments well.

She makes me nervous, but I love when Kat pays attention to me. We sit and talk on the steps of the red-stone Scottish church near Big Trouble House, waiting for Lori to come home from work.

I ask to see her lyrics, finding them complicated, painful, and true. She tells me I am one of the only people who ever asks to read her words.

Blind your mind
So tears will melt.
Numb the place
Where pain is.

She can be so mean.

If I wear clothes that are too similar to hers, she gets really pissed, sarcastic, intending to diminish. "When did you get that dress? That doesn't look like something you would normally wear."

Our styles just cross from time to time. My '70s crochet and chokers and her '60s baby-doll dresses meet at a weird intersection. Like black, over-the-knee socks, for example. I avoid that conflict. When I find vintage silver heart lockets at the thrift store, I give them to her, even though I want them for myself, accepting her as alpha like a puppy rolling over and exposing its belly.

She can be so sweet.

She tells me I make her calm.

She tells me she looks happiest in photos where we're next to each other.

She tells me her mother left her and her father when she was a baby. Her mother wanted to be a hippie instead.

RADIANT ENERGY

Lori. She reminds me of a sunflower. The way those blossoms are the focal point of a bouquet, overpowering in cheer. When you see the sturdy stalk and yellow-fringed blooms, tall and bright, everything seems happier, even when their heavy heads droop like drunk old men.

Her bedroom on the third floor of the Big Trouble House is like an oddities museum filled with small animal skulls, miscellaneous teeth, African masks and carvings. She keeps a real shrunken head boxed in her closet; it's supposed to be a secret, but she shows everyone. It's very real with shriveled skin like smoked meat, long black hair, the mouth stitched shut. A legion of crucifixes shine in her leaded glass window overlooking Colfax Avenue, forming a curtain, the beads jangling and chiming whenever the door is opened or closed. At dusk, you can see swarms of bats flying out of the brick chimney across the street.

Walls covered in band posters and flyers plastered on top of each other, not an inch left bare. Hundreds of bootleg cassette tapes she records at shows. She keeps a tarantula named Riff Raff in a glass cage on her nightstand.

The bed is the heart of the room, where we sit as she shows me all her photos, crying about the people who died or a boy she misses. Many of the photos are of her and someone famous: a young Bruce Springsteen, Iggy Pop, Exene Cervenka from the band X.

She drives a '70s Nova spray-painted black with orange

flames. She usually wears t-shirts, black leggings with cut-off jeans on top, and cowboy boots, although her closet is packed, everything the very best of vintage: a perfect leopard print coat, '50s dresses, Western shirts. Items you know you cannot borrow. A scarab on her forearm and a smiling bat on her shoulder are part of her growing collection of tattoos.

Lori grew up in Minneapolis, but her family moved to suburban Pearl River, New York, when she was a teenager. Her father was vice president of a bank in Manhattan, the city just twenty-five miles away. She ran on the Pearl River Pirates' track and field team with the boys, since there was no girls' team, a skull and crossbones wearing a pirate's hat on her jersey.

Lori worked at Nathan's Famous Coney Island in Nanuet, the next town over. Wednesday was $5-pizza night; she'd make over a hundred pies as well as shuck oysters and cook frog legs, bone cracking when the pelvis broke in two, pulled apart and thrown into the deep fryer. The game room at Nathan's had pinball and a circus video game—a clown jumping on a teeter-totter and popping balloons with his head, a death march playing when he fell off and died. She heard this dirge over and over again during her shifts.

After living on a houseboat in Key West, Florida, after high school, Lori returned to Minneapolis and got a job at the Longhorn, the bar where all the punk bands played. The Longhorn was small and dark like a dungeon. The Suburbs, Suicide Commandos, Loud Fast Rules (who became Soul Asylum), the Replacements, Hüsker Dü—all the iconic Minneapolis bands, always on the calendar. Lori putting down her drink tray to dance, never missing a show, sweating so

Lori in her bedroom at Big Trouble House, 1987

hard that she had to go into the ladies room to wring out her shirt. This is where she met *everybody*, becoming the center of the Minneapolis music scene and beyond. All the touring bands would stay at her house. Anyone she didn't know, she went out of her way to meet in her gregarious, friendly way—whether they were musicians, roadies, or just loved music as much as she did. There's a joke that in her free time, Lori hung out at the Greyhound station asking people if they needed a place to crash.

She is the radio tower, sending radiant energy shimmering through the air.

UNCLEAN

It's been months since the show in the art gallery basement, and we're practicing every day. The crowds are slowly growing, getting into it, yelling things like "Kat scratch fever!" in the middle of our sets. We play little bars, like Fernando's on Lake Street, parties at people's houses. We're constantly on the calendar at 7th Street Entry—now as headliners—and grab weird opening slots at the Cabooze, which is more of a rocker/jam-band bar. We say YES to every offer.

At first I sing one of the songs, but Lori and Kat keep leaving it off the set list.

I want us to play like Soul Asylum does, the way their guitarists rock out back-to-back, but this type of showmanship just isn't our style.

We record our first single, "Dust Cake Boy," for the local label Treehouse Records in a small studio with our friend Brian Paulson, who later becomes a big-deal producer. We don't understand what the fuss is about recording. We just set up our equipment and play together the same as at practice or a live show, getting the songs down in one or two takes.

We're then asked to record a single-of-the-month for the Seattle label Sub Pop, the bitchenest of all independent labels, or so I'm told. I later discover Mudhoney, Tad, L7, Cat Butt, and Nirvana, some of the greatest live bands I've ever seen, also on their roster.

Live, Lori and I keep a steady beat. We rock out fully, hair and bodies dynamic, energy and flow, each of us knowing every single chord, note, and beat in the deepest part of our core. A show on a warehouse loading dock in Northeast Minneapolis: Kat's red guitar with pictures of fat cabbage roses glued on, the kind you could find on a Victorian seed packet. She wears black '30s round-toe shoes, thick-heeled, with swirling patterns embossed in the leather, the ones Lori and I call "polio shoes" behind her back. As we perform, Kat holds one leg back, tiptoe to the ground, leaning forward into the mic, letting out a rattling scream and using a butter knife as a guitar slide, a surprisingly smooth glide up the neck.

She sings about being unclean.

Playing at a warehouse party, 1989

DAY CAMP FOR JEWISH KIDS

At day camp for Jewish kids in third grade, Linda is the girl that everyone wants to be friends with. She has long, dark hair tied in high pigtails, bright yarn hair bows, Izod shirts *and* shorts, a cool red bikini. And she's one of the best swimmers in your age group.

You use toilet paper to make bows for your hair, so everyone calls you "toilet paper head," and that's pretty much the way things are. But you are also a good swimmer, which is why Linda asks you to be her partner. You usually team with Sara, exactly who you don't want to be: goofy red hair that sticks out everywhere, freckles all over her face and body. Sara has big Basset Hound eyes that are always crying about something someone did or said. Her one-piece is all stretched out and so thin that you can see her butt crack.

But you like the Basset Hound girl because she gives you pieces of See's Candies that her aunt brought her from California. You share secrets. Plus, you think the way she is weird looking is actually really cute. Still, when your counselor teams you with Sara instead of Linda, you say, "I don't want to be with her!"

You watch as those big eyes fill.

"I thought you were a nice girl," the counselor says.

Camp photo, 1974

BEAVER LODGE

I move out of the apartment above the CC Club and into a large old house with some of my girlfriends and Grant, who gets his own room in the basement. We call our place the Beaver Lodge. The home dates back to the 1890s, stained glass, wood floors and a little turret, which is my room. Rent is $200 a month.

The turret is charming with wood beams across the ceiling and French doors. I have a futon on the floor and no closet, so my clothes hang on a metal rack and are often full of bees, which enter from a hole in the wall. Fringy shawls for curtains and a few candles on the window ledge. The room is small, so I keep my bass right outside the door, BABES IN TOYLAND written in silver marker on the case.

Many cats live in the Lodge. There are Cake, Nino, Morgana, and Fry. I am very allergic to cats and sneeze all the time, even though I try to keep them out of my room.

The giant open parlor is filled mostly with my parents' old furniture; they built a house on a marsh in Minnetonka and went with neutral decor, discarding the '70s stuff from Hobby Oak Drive. We have the black vinyl bar with gold buttons, and a three-piece wrap-around couch made of velvety green and orange paisley fabric—as kids we could only sit there when we had guests. Since touring bands constantly stay at our place, this piece begins an exciting new life as dirty drummers or bassists traveling through Minneapolis sleep on her textured cushions. Cheese-smelling socks violate her virgin skin. Lead singers' or guitarists' dirty feet are typically found at Big Trouble House, a few blocks away.

Almost any night at the Lodge is movie night: *Faster, Pussycat! Kill! Kill!*, *Beyond the Valley of the Dolls*, kitschy pornos like *Yank My Doodle, It's a Dandy!*, the dirty movies more awkward than funny. The huge living room is always really dark, everyone buried under blankets, eating ice cream and drinking beer. The couch is completely trashed after two years, stuffing gushing from the seams.

Summer afternoons my roommates Katie, Terri, Jill, Jody, Hannah, and I put on our vintage bathing suits, filling up our kiddie pool, sitting in the water, resting our feet sore from waitressing.

"My dogs are barking!"

Green cans of Special Ex, meat on the grill, the neighbor's stinky stare. Unless you have to work, it doesn't matter what time it is. We hang out all day long.

Me, Terri, and Jill, Beaver Lodge housemates, 1988

AS FAR AS YOU CAN GO

As a kid, sitting in the back-back of your family's station wagon, next to the suitcases, building a nest out of blankets. Your brother and sister in the seat in front of you, your dad at the wheel, and mom riding shotgun, reading the map. Driving to Mount Rushmore or Disney World or a dude ranch in Colorado or the Wisconsin Dells. Staying at a 1950s motel with an outdoor swimming pool or a Holiday Inn with a Holidome where you play mini-golf and shuffleboard. Coming home with a beaded belt from Wall Drug, a snow globe of Florida, a straw cowboy hat with a blue star that reads SHERIFF, a keychain from Tommy Bartlett's Robot World.

Head under water, arms and legs fanning out like a frog's, wisps of seaweed brushing your legs, cattails and lily pads, swimming out into the lake as far as you can go before rising for a breath. Floating on your back, staring at the sky.

Corn on the cob and watermelon, Bomb Pops and Creamsicles, hamburgers and chicken drumsticks, shorts and flip-flops and mosquito bites. Sitting on a blanket with your family watching fireworks on the Fourth of July. Running through the sprinklers.

Wearing pajamas and watching a movie while lying on the roof of the car under the starriest sky, bucket of popcorn and a sleeping bag. The big metal speaker, an intermission cartoon where a hot dog does backflips before landing in a bun and inviting you to visit the snack bar. Your mom gives you two dollars. You go to the little brick building to buy a treat and see all the other kids wearing their pj's too.

THREE OWLS

Promoting only our singles, Babes in Toyland hit the road. Our first stop is Madison, Wisconsin. We sing the Muppets' "Mahna Mahna" song when we pass the town of Menomonie, not knowing that years later we'd still be silently mouthing that chorus to each other.

Lori books the tours, placing endless phone calls, jotting down places, numbers, and dates in a notebook, making the most of her personal connections. She is our manager, too, taking care of the cash, which makes sense because she is good at saving, while Kat and I immediately spend whatever we have.

It's garage sales for gas money, traveling with socks in a grocery bag if I don't have time to pack. It's sleeping on strangers' floors. If no one offers us a place, we stay in our cargo van, nicknamed Vanna White, parking at rest areas or truck stops in the middle of nowhere, hanging out on the roof of the van in our sleeping bags and falling asleep as the stars shine in a boundless sky. Or all three of us tucked into a pillowy nest up in the "loft"—a sleeping shelf in the van's cargo area made from scrap boards to hide our equipment and get us off the metal cargo floor. It's hot up there, built too close to the felty ceiling, no room to move, no air. Lori grinds her teeth in her sleep next to my head. In the morning, gas station bathrooms: washing armpits in the sink, changing underwear in the stall.

We know way too much about each other.

Each day you find out who's going to be fun and who's going to suck. We take turns playing those roles. The worst is knowing you suck most of all.

We never think about recording contracts, magazine covers, or big dollars. Breaking even is OK. Free pizza from the promoter is even better. Fifty dollars, just enough to get to the next stop, is standard. We are three owls, looking around from a tree, our world surreal, manic, in constant motion.

Grant and I break up because we both make out with other people too many times. It started out as just what he did, which really made me sad, but then it ended up being my thing too. It's good to be free.

Kat doesn't drive because she lost her license: intoxication, belligerence, night in jail. She usually rides shotgun, refusing to sit in back because it's windowless with an exhaust problem that makes you sick. "The Vomit Chamber." Lori and I take turns, when the other is driving, sitting on the floor of the chamber or lying down in the loft.

We call the passenger side "The Princess Seat" behind Kat's back.

Lori is always mad at me. I have a few guesses why. Because of my allergies, I don't want to stay at houses where there are cats, and almost everyone has a cat; I want to stay at motels, even though we can't afford them; I don't always party, because I am introverted, often preferring to be alone, and also because I love to sleep; on long drives, I am the one who always needs to stop to eat or pee, and I am not patient about it.

But mostly Lori seems mad for no reason. She snarls at both of us in the van, then walks into the club and is all sunshine to everyone new. She stays permanently angry

Kat in the front seat of Vanna White, 1989

when I use borrowed band money and trade in my small Peavey amp to buy a giant, no-brand cabinet with four fifteen-inch speakers and a Sunn bass head, the set-up we call "The Refrigerator" because of its comparable weight. Kat and I think it looks and sounds badass, but we can't get it up steps ourselves. Lori puts on a stink face when she has to help carry it.

Still, most the time things are pretty righteous. We don't have to stop at the bank or clean our apartments or make appointments for anything at all. We don't have to go to work or set the alarm or brush our hair or change our clothes if we don't want to. Drinking beer in the morning is socially acceptable and often helpful in making you feel better than before.

We read magazines on the way to the shows (never using the word *gig*), really bad ones like *Star* or *Weekly World News,* or if we're in a serious mood, *Spin* or *Rolling Stone.*

Eating beef jerky, sunflower seeds, raw corn from farm stands. All three of us loving canned sardines and smoked oysters—less than two dollars a can—peeling open the tins inside the van is strictly prohibited. Pouring the oil onto the pavement, watching it flow shiny streams. We stop at grocery stores in small towns; managers follow us around full of suspicions that never pay off. I gain fifteen pounds in one month from eating candy bars every time we stop, the weight made more obvious by my new super-short haircut that takes forever to grow out.

Collecting souvenirs like aviator sunglasses embossed with the American flag, shot glasses, and state magnets for each place we play. Eventually, I nearly have them all. All our crap takes up the foot room of the van, crammed into every last bit of space. The unread books: Nick Cave's biography and Leonard Cohen's poetry. Lori's records and posters; the red, white, and blue stars-and-stripes roller-skate case where I keep my tuner and cords. Our clothes: long vintage dresses cut with scissors, crooked and a little too short, all of Lori's boots. A giant cardboard box filled with merch, always in the way. T-shirts saying I'M WITH STUPID on the front, a drawing of a finger pointing up to your face, quality of a jailhouse tattoo, BABES IN TOYLAND on the back. Lori ordered five hundred of those without asking us because some guy she liked drew that shit—Kat and I bitch about this behind her back. We sell those shirts for years sitting at some folding table or the side of the stage, Kat and I with stinky looks on our faces whenever we take out the box.

Late nights at roadside restaurants, we are seated in the back. The truck drivers stare at us heaping our plates at the salad bar and have no idea what to make of such

Sleeping in the "Vomit Chamber" of Vanna White as Lori drives, 1989

raggedy-ass girls, especially Lori's long hair that's now become dreadlocks. Kat saves her money by not ordering food, but then asks for bites of ours, which Lori and I bitch about behind her back.

We play in New Orleans. Hardly anyone comes to the show, but I am enchanted by the city, so sultry and mystic. The buildings all seem to have a story. We walk around the French Quarter and talk to an old street musician who says, "Your butt is too big to be a bass player."

The van breaks down often. My dad sends money to get us back on the road. We use our tattered road atlas to locate the Western Union in some bummer town. Vanna, she smells like wet rug, sour milk, face powder, and girl, the air blending and trailing out into the valleys, plains, rivers, swamps, mountains, and pastures as we pass on our way anywhere.

I LIVE INSIDE

When we perform live we don't just make sound. The music removes the hiss of static, X-rays spirit, creates energy. It is color, air, emotion, all I ever want to be.

The feelings rise in my stomach before we go on, not nerves, but anxious like a filly at the starting gate needing to run around the track. When I close my eyes on stage I can see the light shining through my lids; the skin and veins like a baby bird filter luminescence. The beams cutting through the dark to the stage, the strangeness of being lit. In a big club, you can only see the people in the first few rows: the guy with a backpack who gives you a copy of his fanzine, the woman covered in tattoos, long-haired boys staring softly, the girl with braces on her teeth. When they start dancing, that exertion feeds yours, currents moving back and forth, undistilled, sincere.

7th Street Entry, 1989

The three of us create heavenly heat. The movement of the big bones of our legs, small bones of fingers, hearts circulating with blood, heads shaking off fragmented thoughts. All that we love channels above us as we play.

A trio of ghostly vapors tangling together, rising.

7th Street Entry, 1989

NOT NAKED

I stare at Kat. She has an eye tic and blinks a lot, like the world hurts to look at. When we're in Minneapolis she works as a stripper at the Belmont in St. Paul. I pick her up there before practice sometimes. It is so dark, the old men, blue light, the glue-like smell. She carries her outfits in a vintage suitcase. When the guys by the stage make gross comments, she steps on their fingers with her black tap shoes.

I never watch her dance but ask lots of questions. She is direct and usually patient with me. I want to know what she shows. What happens in the booths. How much money do you make? Is it itchy to shave down there? Do you get nervous? What's it like?

Sometimes she has bruises on her legs from falling down, running into things, wasted.

"It turns into not naked after a while, in your mind. You have to drink a lot first."

I get drunk one night with some strangers and use this line, telling them I'm a stripper. I want to be that girl in the movie *Betty Blue*, all fucked up like that.

She always makes me feel like a fraud. By she, of course, I mean me.

THE BUS STOP

We arrive in Madison, park the van, and go into the club. In the daytime these bars make me feel lousy; black walls, sticky pay phones, always smelling like puke. You are not supposed to see that shit in the light. But we dig playing at O'Cayz Corral, because Cay, the owner, makes us spaghetti. We sit at the bar and eat before the place opens.

We're on the bill with the Membranes, a punk band from England. Both bands stay at our friend Amy's house. We all go back to O'Cayz the next night, some cover band scheduled. The bartender calls in sick, so the promoter asks us all to work behind the bar. We give our customers whatever they want, don't ask anyone to pay—like we're throwing a party. I feel bad giving away Cay's booze for a minute, but it's so fun I can't stop. We make lots of tips. When the place closes, we fill empty beer bottles with peppermint schnapps and head to the beach.

One of the Membranes crew knows how to breathe fire. He has all the gear and teaches us how to do it. Giant flames light our faces as the lake shines behind us, the constellations sparkle above. Minty bottles and the sand under our bare feet. We shout into the peaceful night.

In the morning, I wake up outside on Amy's front porch, a busy neighborhood, home close to the sidewalk.

The boys from the Membranes are in sleeping bags next to me, only messy punk hair showing out the top. I sit up and look around. There's a bus stop about fifteen

Friends welcome us on the road, 1989

feet away, people waiting to go to work. It's so early. The sun hurts my eyes. The bus stop people look at me and I look at them; we all feel sorry for each other.

A neatly dressed lady in her thirties asks, "Are you all right? Do you need some help?"

"No, thanks," I say with hangover-soaked disinterest, dragging my sleeping bag inside the dark house, crumpling into a vacant couch and going back to sleep.

MY BABY-STYLE RAGE

I am starving, but Lori and Kat aren't eating anything except sharing a big bag of potato chips and don't care about real food today. We're in the middle of a long drive. They think the next city is not too far for me to wait to stop, even though that is still an hour and a half away.

"Can't I just run quickly into the next gas station and get some crackers or something?"

The answer is "No," and I am filled with hate for everything and everyone. I sit up too quickly and hit my head on the ceiling of the van. Hard. Further inciting my baby-style rage.

"Are you OK?"

"Just don't even talk to me," I say.

In the loft of Vanna White, 1989

Mother

Mother
This is my life
Sister
Come and take my life
You are obscene and you know it
I run from me and it shows
That's what you like me for, huh, sister
Crawling now on the floor

57

RICKETS AND SCURVY

I am not involved in scheduling the tours. It is a better fit for me to just play the bass. I trust that Lori knows what to do and who to play with. This does not stop me from complaining when the drives are long, the billings appear random, or the pay seems low.

As our popularity grows, handling all the bookings becomes too much work for Lori, so we hire a booking agent. Now there is someone else to get pissed at when we have to travel a thousand miles for a $75 guarantee. We feel like we are at the point where we can be more selective, but we still get those kinds of shows.

Our agent gets really mad at promoters and yells at them on the phone. "Your booking agent is a dick" is something we hear a lot. It's embarrassing, but also good. Like when we get pizza every night when our contract specifies that they provide us dinner. It's nice to have someone else advocate for us.

"Tell them we need real food, like fruits and vegetables."

We feel shitty all the time due to hangovers, zero mental stimulation, and lack of sleep and exercise (van ass). Eating pizza every day is making it worse.

"We're going to get rickets and scurvy," we say.

The tours feel endless, but making friends with the other bands as we travel from town to town together is boss. It's like the first day of school, when you are a little cautious with the other kids at first but then become best friends. We ride in each other's vans and hang out late and go to bars and parties where we'll occasionally set up our equipment and rock again. Sometimes I go to bed early, and there is usually another person who is the same way. They become my not-as-fun-as-everybody-else friends.

Our tour with Cows is a blast, even though there's hardly anybody at the shows. Their music is discordant and demented, really noisy yet somehow accessing a pleasing place in my brain. And our good friend Katie from the Beaver Lodge is along selling merch. She brings a calm vibe, and also loves to drive; these two elements help make this tour a breeze. When we play with Cows in Houston, there is a cold spell and it's freezing in the unheated club. The promoter brings out a giant propane heater and we perform in coats and hats and scarves in front of an audience of three people. Doing goofy vaudeville-style dances—the

Cows performing, 1989. Tony, the drummer, has a mop on his head, like Lori's hair.

kind like you are running while waving—to crack each other up while we rock in our woolens. Daring each other to sniff their singer Shannon's red cowboy hat, the one he wears every day. It smells really bad in there, much worse than the black velvet and white lace–collared dress Kat constantly wears.

CRAZY FOR BOYS ALL DAY LONG

When we don't have a floor to sleep on, Kevin, the bass player of Cows, and I check into cheap motels, telling the desk clerks we're married. Then everyone else sneaks in, all tiptoe and shhhh-finger to lips in the middle of the night, ten of us in one room. When their drummer, Tony, and I catch really bad colds, we earn one of the beds. I go take cough syrup in the middle of the night in the crappy bathroom and find cockroaches on it. Sleeping all stiff in our clothes, making sure not to touch each other as we cough and blow our noses, lest the other think we have sexy on the mind.

Some midwestern town with Tad (a band and also the singer's name) and Laughing Hyenas, who have this female guitarist who is like an even tougher Kat and a bassist with a beard like the Amish. Tad tells me that I look like the actress Shelley Duvall and keeps calling me Olive Oyl, the character she plays in the movie *Popeye*.

We also tour with God Bullies from Michigan. Their singer, Mike, dresses like a priest on stage and makes motions with his tie like he is hanging himself—this freaks me out every time. The God Bullies live in a trailer park in Kalamazoo, up on bluffs that overlook a lake, and we stay with them. We have a bonfire and take long walks in this beautiful and serene place. I hang out in the singer's trailer and we pretend to be Loretta Lynn and her husband. He

Babes in Toyland with The Jesus Lizard and our friend John Joyce, 1989

tells me to get him beer. I say, "You never let me go out and have any fun."

We also perform some East Coast shows with The Jesus Lizard from Chicago. Their music is noisy, too, but also complicated and evocative. The first night, the drummer, Mac, says we should wrestle someday because "Even if I lose, I win." I get this huge crush on him, always putting my sleeping bag next to his when we stay on people's floors. But he won't make out with me. When I get Kat to ask him why, he says something like, "I don't want to get into anything unless I know it's forever." Then he makes out with other girls. Then why'd you say the thing about wrestling? But they remain one of my very favorite bands, and the singer, David, literally takes his balls out on stage every single night when they play the song "Tight and Shiny."

The promoters often put us on stupid bills with just any girl band, even if they are country or '70s rock or metal or blues. Because we're girls and they're girls. But mostly it's all guys around on the road. I wish I could focus on music and stop being crazy for boys all day long. Wanting so badly to be one of those aloof and mysterious girls who are unattainable. The kind you pursue and respect. But I'm pretty easy sometimes, mostly when I drink. When I don't get the attention of men, I feel empty, inferior, and alone.

FANCY PANTY OIL

"Dust Cake Boy" is getting played on college radio stations. There are more people at the shows every time we return to a town, and we travel most of the year. The tours are hardcore, grueling, playing every night for up to eight weeks straight. At first my fingers blister, then bleed. I play with them wrapped in tape. Eventually they callous and I am set free from the pain. Our friend Howard comes along and sells merch. We hope we can afford to bring our own soundman along soon too.

Picking up Kat to leave for tour, Lori honks the horn from the street. Kat looks out her window, comes downstairs, and gets in the van. She smells like frangipani oil, which she calls "fancy panty oil." Howard calls it "Love's Baby Soft on crack." She has a vintage makeup case, part of a suitcase set, filled with face creams, stray beat-up tampons, unopened herbal remedies, Throat Coat tea.

She disappears a lot, returning out of it and with sketchy people. There's always an excuse.

We understand the problem is drugs, but the actual use takes place out of sight. Sometimes it feels like Lori and I are more annoyed with Kat than worried about her, like the times when she isn't home when we try to pick her up for practice. Yet deep down we fear for her safety and want to help. I have a mothering style and Lori is more of a hard-ass about it. We both know that the band is what gives Kat a sense of purpose, people she is accountable to and who care about her. It's part of our life and career, something we are accustomed to and never talk about. With Kat, that is.

PENISES I NEVER WANTED TO SEE

I wake up to him breathing on my face.

You could tell he was conflicted about our staying at his house after the show; supercharged insistence that we come over mixed with numerous references to his place being really messy. But we ignore his cues. We are broke and have nowhere else to go.

He makes it clear that no one is allowed to sleep on his bed. As soon as we arrive, Kat passes out there, wasted. She lies on top of the tangled sheets, her pretty dress hiked up, triangle of panty exposed. I'm sleeping on the couch, Lori on the floor. In most houses where we stay, the bed is considered the best spot, the couch second, floors third. But this apartment is life-gone-wrong, nothing bohemian about it: dirty kitchen with cheap cabinets and linoleum floors stained with salsa, a tiny bathroom with standing water and pubes in the tub, a lonely cat mewing. Here, my spot on the couch covered with a Mexican blanket doesn't really qualify for second. Everyone loses.

Howard says, "Oh no, not me," when he walks in and goes to sleep in the van parked curbside in the questionable neighborhood. Lori and I watch TV with our host in the dark living room for a bit. Pretty soon he leaves, something drug occurring.

He is easy to picture out there on the street, red-faced, dirty hair thin and curly. Howard sees him talking on a pay phone, adamant, wearing old wing tip shoes without socks, a beat-up motorcycle jacket somehow not rock or vintage.

I sleep in the sweaty clothes I wore playing the show. This is no place to disrobe. I doze, but wake up sneezing and itching from the cat. The guy keeps coming back to the house, then leaving again. With Kat on his bed and me on the couch, he has no place to sit or sleep.

He is a musician, which gets many men laid, but this one is unpopular with the ladies. His unpopularity has to do with his face.

The face that is breathing on me as I wake up on his skanky couch.

His fingers run through my hair. He is kneeling beside me, petting my head. Also muttering, drunk and angry, mostly crazy, something about me and the Queen of England.

Because I tell him to stop, he thinks I'm uptight. Like the Queen of England.

He goes into the bedroom. There is more stumbling, things being dropped, muttering, then the unmistakable sound of ferocious masturbation. I open one eye and see this happening through the open bedroom door: his back, dick in hand, the motion. I close my eyes tight and pull my sleeping bag over my head.

Lori dreams peacefully, snoring softly. Kat is in a deep drunken slumber lying on her back.

It doesn't take long for him to finish. He again exits the house.

"Lori, wake up."

"Lori!"

I tell her what happened and that I want to leave. But she is comfy and tired, getting up and going is too much work. She says I can get into her sleeping bag with her. That option is not appealing either.

I try to wake up Kat, somehow thinking she'll understand my urgency.

She sits up, legs out, body upright, hair in face.

"Nice doggy," she says to the cat and flops back down.

"Lori, we can't stay here, we gotta go before he gets back."

Lori finally agrees, getting freaked out too. Now there is no way to leave fast enough. *He's going to catch us sneaking out, hurry, come on! Let's go.*

We grab our stuff, sleeping bags over shoulders, one of us on each side of Kat, our arms looped around hers as we drag her out the door. The chaos of the scene makes us giggly, frantic, energized. A team.

We get in the van, and Howard asks, "What the fuck?" *Jacking off, super fucking creepy, hurry, let's go.*

Allergies fully ignited, I have hives, toilet paper inserted in both nostrils. Still I drive, which I almost never do late at night because I am a baby about that kind of thing; I hate to drive any time of the day. But this is part of the deal to get Lori to agree to leave, promising to drive to the next town. I will travel all night and all day to get far away from this place.

We get to a stoplight a few blocks away and see the guy walking down the middle of the street. A lummox, tall and staggering, lit by street light. He sees us too. Even Kat is alert now, and all four of us scream as we swerve around him. He makes eye contact as we pass.

I grab a smoke from the worn-out pack of menthols I carry, one pack usually lasting me a couple weeks. We have no destination except the next town, where we don't need to be for several days. We just sleep in the van along the way.

I'm at the wheel again two nights later, and in the darkness of night, we stop at a gas station. There's just a booth where you pay, a friendly guy behind the counter, sodas, a few off-brand snacks. I get a key on a giant ring and go out to the bathroom in a separate building.

As I walk back to the vehicle, the attendant yells, "Hey! What are you doing?"

I am confused. He knows exactly what I'm doing; he just gave me the key. I look up and see his penis hanging out the open fly of his work pants as he smiles proudly at me. I run to the van, start it up, roll down the window, throw the bathroom key on the ground, honk the horn, hard, repeatedly, yelling "Motherfucker!" as we squeal out and back onto the highway.

Guitars, drums, and amps rattle in the back.

The girls are soon sound asleep. Howard stays up, sitting in front with me. He offers a sip of his soda and some off-brand chips, which I accept. He says that was the most swears he's ever heard in a row. We talk about the possibility of UFOs landing in open fields like the ones we are passing. We drive.

COOL AS FUCK

The most recent East Coast tour is stellar. We perform at some of our favorite venues like The Middle East in Boston. The promoter, Billy Ruane, wears a trench coat and has wild messy hair. He jumps on stage while we rock, doing these jumps that are both rock and karate, somersaulting on the ground. Even if no one shows up, he pays a lot of money—which we learn is out of his pocket—and buys tons of merch. He feeds us really well, too, because the place is also a Middle Eastern restaurant. We go nuts for free falafel and hummus. We stay with a friend in a huge art loft with an abundance of second-hand couches. We dig Boston.

Maxwell's in Hoboken, New Jersey, is another excellent stop. All the bands we meet on the road tell us how great it is to play at Maxwell's, and they are correct. The promoter buys dinner at their Italian restaurant in the room next to the club, and you get to order whatever you want from the actual menu, like fancy pasta or mussels. On tour, eating is the second most important thing to rocking, and this is the best food you get on tour. The actual shows are not super packed, but the crowd is always there especially to see the band, standing up front by the stage, talking to you after. Also, it's really close to New York, but no one breaks into your van and steals all your stuff like they do in Manhattan. The last time we were in New York, at the Pyramid Club, someone stole our bags after we loaded in our gear, leaving broken glass and blood in the vehicle. Lori had her stuff with her, but all of Kat's and my best things were gone. Kat found some of her clothes being sold on the street and took them back, but I had only what I was wearing. In the next town, we stopped at a thrift store where I bought one red flowered sundress that I wore every day.

Still, despite the thievery, it's hard not to feel like you are in the center of the universe when you are in New York. Playing at the punk club CBGB, which is sort of like any other venue, dark and dirty, but there is a feel to it that is somehow darker and dirtier and more full of meaning than anyplace else. I'd read about the venue in *Trouser Press*, *NME* from England, and other music magazines as the place where the Ramones, Blondie, and Talking Heads got their starts, so it feels important playing here, and the room gets pretty full. The crowd is enthusiastic and engaged, dancing hard when we go on at 1 a.m.

We stay with another friend who lives on Avenue C, where tons of junkies hang out, so we have to carry our gear, including The Refrigerator, up three flights of stairs to her 300-square-foot apartment so it doesn't get stolen too.

Some of the bands we play with a lot on the road are the Melvins, Surgery, Unsane, Urge Overkill, and the Didgits. They're all hard rockers, punk or alternative I guess you'd call them. The touring circuit is pretty tight and you end up on bills with a lot of the same bands, so you make a lot of friends. We leave each other notes in marker on the walls of the dressing rooms.

But best of all, we love returning and playing anywhere in our hometown. The crowds full of our friends and my family; my brother when he is in town, which is not often since he travels as a stand-up comedian, and my

On tour promoting our first two singles, 1989

mom, who wears earplugs and stands proudly backstage. Since my sister is ten years older, her life is so different: husband, small children, and responsibilities. They never say it to me, but I think our music is too psycho for her and my dad—they're hardly ever at our shows, yet they still communicate their love and support, so I don't mind. And there's my mom, side stage at the Old Avalon Theater in Minneapolis, a former porno movie place, where we're opening for White Zombie, this rocking metal band from New York with tons of hair and a kickass female bassist. They invite us on stage to sing the Kiss song "Dr. Love" for their encore. Since my mom just left, I do a shot before we go on and feel cool as fuck.

LEON STINKS

That morning you tried to curl your hair to make it feather, but that look doesn't really work on Jewish girls' hair (curly, frizzy, berserk), so it's sticking out. You also cut your own bangs, trying to be in style, and got into trouble from your mom for that. And the bangs make the hairdo much worse. You're in fifth grade choir class. It is right before lunch and hard to concentrate because you can smell pizza muffins and canned corn, your favorites, from the cafeteria a few doors away.

You took choir because all your best girlfriends did, but you don't really like it. You think it's weird, like watching musicals, it seems so fake when they sing instead of talk.

The class is singing Blood, Sweat & Tears' "Spinning Wheel."

What goes up must come down.
Spinning wheel got to go round.

Practicing for the spring concert, the class is supposed to look up and down along with the lyrics, which makes the whole thing extra stupid.

"Ms. Leon, stop mouthing the words," the teacher says.

"I wasn't mouthing!" you say, even though you were.

You have to sit out in the hall and you pretend you think it's funny, telling the teacher, "I don't care," as you head out the door. But once you're out in the hall and it's just you sitting on a plastic chair, it feels pretty sad. You can hear them inside, singing about painted ponies.

You think about the big cartoon foot that squashes people on *Monty Python's Flying Circus* so you won't cry.

Before this year, you never thought about hairdos or clothes styles, but now the girls are starting to pick on you for that stuff. So you tell your mom, "No more Garanimals. I want Izods."

When class is over, you wait for your friends, but they walk past you.

"Hi," you say, but they act like they don't hear you.

You go to lunch and see your friends; you say, "Hi," again, but still they don't answer. You sit by them anyway. They turn away. You try to eat your pizza muffin but aren't hungry anymore. When they are all done eating, you follow them out into the hall, and the most popular girl says, "Hey, I left my sweater in the lunchroom. Will you go get it?"

"Sure!"

"We'll wait right here for you."

But you don't see her sweater. You go back into the hall and they are all gone. When you walk to your locker, you see all the girls standing there, shoving in a note. They look at you and start laughing, then run away. You look at the piece of paper. There's a drawing of you with your hair beserking and smell waves coming from a stick body wearing stupid overalls like the ones you have on. The picture is titled "Leon Stinks," a goof on the boxer Leon Spinks. Underneath, it says, "Nobody likes you."

THE DRUMSTICK DEBACLE

Driving all night to play back-to-back shows 650 miles apart. Kat and I ask Lori if we can have an extra $5 or $10 after we spend all our money; this time, she says yes. I find out that sometimes they both get extra money but don't give me any. Then we get into a fight.

"You know, my parents are the ones who have our van on their insurance," I say.

"Well, then let's just pay them back so you'll stop talking about that."

"I guess that's your way of saying *thanks*."

Lori does most of the driving, smoking with the windows barely cracked, listening to super-loud hardcore when we just woke up, creating a torture chamber that travels across many lands. When I offer to drive, she usually says no but then bitches about us not helping. OK, it's true: I occasionally use a pretend I-am-mostly-asleep voice when I offer to take over at the wheel late at night. But this has been a really long tour. When Kat complains about our driving styles—Lori goes fast and swerves around people; I'm like an old guy, slow and steady goes it—we remind her of the fact that she doesn't have a license. Lori and I agree that the non-driver has forfeited her right to an opinion.

For the sake of disclosure, I need to mention that last week, after we stopped for gas in the middle of the night, I got on the interstate and drove the wrong direction for two hours before realizing it. We were really late to our show.

Lori in the loft of Vanna White, 1989

How many times can you say you're sorry?

But it's time to shut down that wrong-way-highway thought loop that keeps spinning in my brain. At the club, the promoter offers to take us to the music store so Kat and I can get new strings. I'm hoping he will also offer to buy us something delicious for dinner.

"Lori, we're going to get strings. Do you want to go with?"

"No," she says, but I know she's not listening, she's talking to the lead singer of the headlining band, telling him the same stupid jokes we've heard a million times before. And I just heard her tell him that she *always* has to do *all* the driving, knowing I can hear her. I am trying to be mature.

"Do you want us to get you anything?"

"No," she says without even looking at me as she gives him a high five.

At the music store, Kat and I sign concert posters for the staff and they give us a sweet deal. We consider getting Lori drumsticks because we figure she needs them. Fuck that, we decide. She should've come with.

That night, Lori asks why I didn't get her drumsticks after she hears about the sweet deal.

"You said you didn't need anything," I say, thinking it's your own dumbass fault.

"You knew I needed drumsticks!"

She is really pissed.

"I asked if you wanted anything, so you forfeited your right to be mad when you said you didn't want to come with," I say.

I look right at her and she looks right back at me, the fire of anger in our eyes. So begins resentment that lasts for weeks and the spinning of a brand-new thought loop in my underused brain.

HER SCARIEST LOUD WHISPER

I hear that Lori calls me "Kat's puppet" behind my back, but I don't see it that way. I just agree with Kat more than I do with her. Lori is more punk rock than me. I like a little luxury whenever possible. Mostly, she doesn't like spending money and holds onto all of our cash. Kat agrees with me most of the time, except when she is too wasted to care or talking to Lori, who she then agrees with instead of me. It would be sweet to not lay my eyes on either of them for a while.

We're at another club. I'm sitting at the bar drinking a bloody mary and reading the local weekly as we wait for soundcheck. This quiet moment is sacred to me, a form of solitude that is especially fine as the vodka quiets my addled mind.

There's this version of myself that I access in my mind who never complains. She recognizes that my life has so many gifts, being in this band and seeing the whole country. She knows how incredibly lucky I am. I think of those motivational speakers who tell you to visualize who you want to be, and how you can make that happen. I want to be warm and kind and open to everyone, like Lori, who is so charming to strangers that all of her goodness gets used up, and there is nothing left but her husk, and then she is such a total fucking bitch to me and Kat. Take a deep breath. We all have our struggles. *But I still hate her!* Let it go. *But I asked if she wanted anything at the music store and she said no!* Let it go.

This guy sits down next to me. I'm thinking please don't talk to me, but he does. I tell myself to be nice, and really, you've never seen such a friendly person. He tells me all about his life, how he has a band too. He buys me another drink. I answer all his questions.

"Where do you play next?"

"I don't remember." I am not even sure which dull-as-shit town this is now. I would ask Lori, who remembers these things, but we're not talking. Kat knows even less than I do.

"Where did you play last night?"

I don't know the answer to that one either.

This conversation is boring, so I excuse myself to go to the bathroom, praying it's one stall so I can lock the door and pee alone.

Dang! Two stalls. But at least no one else is in here; that's what I'm thinking as someone walks in. This woman, staring at me with great loathing. I have no idea why she hates me, but for a moment I imagine that Lori told her to. Now she is yelling at me, freaking out, and it's as arbitrary and liquor-soaked as it sounds. She tells me she loves her boyfriend and that I should leave him alone. It takes a second to realize that she is talking about the guy at the bar. I am almost crying from all this insane bellowing, and the lousy version of myself starts winning.

You know I'm in a band, right? That means I can get boys way hotter than your boring-as-fuck boyfriend. I was only talking to him because I am so motherfucking friendly, and maybe if you had your own band he would want to talk to you instead of me.

Kat spending "alone time" at the bar

That's what I want to say, but all I can do is stammer, "We were just talking…"

I get out of there and tell Kat what happened. She's sitting on the barstool the farthest point away from mine; we understand alone time. She goes into the bathroom, where the yeller still lingers, now with two of her friends. Kat says all those things I wish I'd said as I stand behind her, and then adds this, using her scariest loud whisper, close to the girl's face:

"Don't fuck with my bass player."

The girl throws a beer bottle at her boyfriend during the first song of our set and gets dragged out of the bar by the bouncer. Lori and I look at each other and smile.

ASLEEP IN THEIR BEDS

Even after playing together for years, I feel anxious around Lori and Kat, never completely at ease. Sometimes Kat comes up behind me and puts her arms around my waist, lifting me up. Like we are the kind of friends found in an alternate universe, living normal lives; this means a lot to me. But I can never say the right thing to her. I always feel like a dumb kid. Lori embarrasses me when she is loud and inconsiderate, saying "fuck" or "cunt" at a restaurant, seated next to kids.

Driving at night, approaching a town. Lights in the distance, little stars, red towers, a factory with smoke flowing from the chimney like a locomotive. Everyone asleep in their beds. Sitting in the back of the van, I pull my sweatshirt hood down low on my forehead, draw the strings tight, turn on my Walkman and listen to Nick Drake, Led Zeppelin, Big Star. White headlights rush past us in the dark, red taillights to follow or pass. Watching the years go by. Night becomes day, seasons change, farmland turns to desert.

Vanna White, rolling down the highway, 1989

WHAT'S WRONG WITH THE WORLD

We arrive in Minneapolis as the sun comes up and get stuck in a traffic jam. "This is what's wrong with the world; everyone gets up too early, sits in traffic, and works at jobs they hate. That's why they're so mad all the time," Howard says as we return from tour. When you're in a band, it's like experiencing years' worth of life and fun and parties and new people every day. Over and over again. It must be so boring to be normal.

Even though we have just spent a month together in a van, instead of going home, unpacking, doing laundry, taking naps, we head directly to the CC Club. We cram into a vinyl booth and order bloody marys. They have "Dust Cake Boy" on the jukebox. I read *City Pages* and *The Reader*, the two Minneapolis weekly papers, to check out what's going on around town, circling shows I want to see.

Going to see Run Westy Run and dancing until my feet hurt from being stepped on in the dense crowd, getting burned by a cigarette and soaked from a spilled beer. Not caring as the singer swings from the pipes while everyone goes apeshit.

On Sundays, after bar close, we go to Joe's Chicken Shack because they stay open until 1 a.m. when everyone else closes at midnight. They serve only 3.2 beer, not full strength. It doesn't matter. Pool and $3 pitchers and hanging with all our friends. Then a party at someone's house; whoever's at Joe's is invited. Everyone living in big old

Katie, Kat, and me at Beaver Lodge, 1989

houses, four or five roommates, these beautiful old places with super-cheap rent. Jamming with our friends in the basement; there seem to be amps and a drum kit in every single one. Everyone watching as if it were a real show.

It's good to be home even though Minneapolis is gloomy in the winter. There's a connection between the weather and the art scene—something unique, special, and hard to pinpoint, something inspiring. The cold acts as a conduit. The loneliness and isolation are intense, inspiring creativity and friendship, an adventure just going outside. You become addicted to both the triumph and the melancholy.

Being home, wearing pj's, sipping tea, and watching a movie feels extra good. The way the world looks black and white, driving by a figure at the bus stop bundled in a parka, hunched down keeping his or her face out of the wind, the snowflakes blow by like a dream. There is so much to feel.

Autumn leaves and spring lilacs. The summers burst with sunflowers and bike rides and barbecues. Minneapolis is filled with lakes, right in the middle of the city, plus the Mississippi River, which looks most beautiful as you cross the Hennepin Avenue Bridge, passing the vintage Grain Belt Beer and Gold Medal Flour signs.

SHADOWS AND FLASHES OF SKIN

It's summer, so we go to Hidden Beach. Some people call it "Bare Ass Beach," but only occasionally do you witness nudity in the daytime. But tons of people skinny-dip at night, in the dark only shadows and flashes of skin. There is also a mud pit to sit in and come out covered, but I never want to do that. I'd rather swim, backstroke, staring at the sky. Underwear and bra since I am not all naked and free, not gonna let some random dude take a peek.

At Hidden Beach after one of our shows, all of our boyfriends are the best guys from the bar and we ride on the backs of their motorcycles to get there. We'll pick up our stuff and the van in the morning. Couples are sneaking off into the woods. Some forty-year-old guy tags along and plays a bongo.

I get home before sunrise with a damp boy. Sand peppers the flowered sheets and patchwork quilt, wet clothes all over the room, taken off in a big hurry. *Exile on Main Street*, burning candles, and drinking red wine. Waking up with the futon halfway across the room. In the morning, the long-haired boy sleeps as I make coffee, young peachy skin, the ones that always seem to go to the shows alone.

SLEEPOVER CAMP

Making candleholders by gluing shells and colored glass onto coffee cans, looping yarn around popsicle sticks for God's eyes, an ashtray for your parents, even though they don't smoke. They can use it for guests.

At camp that year after seventh grade, there is one other girl in your cabin who no one talks to. Her name is Wendy. You both are bashful at first but bond over having the same favorite book, *Where the Red Fern Grows* by Wilson Rawls, a bittersweet fable about two dogs, Old Dan and Little Ann. When Old Dan dies, Little Ann lies at his grave and dies of heartbreak; it is in this spot that the rare red fern grows, a symbol of true love.

Wendy is the same amount dorky as you are, but her problem is having short hair and not looking good that way, while your problem is being undersized and Jewish. You are exactly like the caricature sketched during your family trip to the Catskills: your head twice the size of your body, giant eyes and teeth popping out of your head as you play the piano. With your curly hair grown halfway down your back, you are a scrawny wolf-girl.

In elementary school, you had something going for you: being a really fast runner and getting picked first when kids chose teams. You were also a good gymnast, competing on the high school team while you were still in junior high. This is why you picked trampoline as your morning activity at camp, where you meet a girl named Jessie. She is a year older and pretty in a bad-girl-smoking-cigarettes way. You become friends when you are the only ones who can do backflips on the tramp. You realize she is exactly the kind of girl you could be. Jessie, who brought her crimping iron along and does your hair. Deep down you always knew there was no way you could ever be popular, and it is surprisingly easy to let go of that dream. Being bad sounds even better.

You have a free hour to do anything you want in the afternoons, and you start going to Jessie's cabin. Jessie doesn't have that many friends either, but it never seems to bother her. You realize you don't want to be friends with boy-hair Wendy from your cabin anymore. You pretend not to see her when free time starts and you head quickly down the wooded path.

Up on Jessie's top bunk, you look through issues of this magazine from England called *Trouser Press*. She tells you about all the bands. Leafing through the pages, staring at pictures of Adam Ant. He is so sexy in his Paul Revere frilly shirt, the white streak of makeup across his face, a pirate hat. She has a cassette deck and plays his songs for you. This music is beautiful, the kind of songs only you and your best friend Jessie can understand, with the tribal beats and the yodelly singing, and the other girls in her cabin saying, "That music is so weird! Turn it off!" But you don't turn it off, because this time, you know they're the ones who are wrong.

BONA FIDE

Twin/Tone, the Minneapolis label that put out albums by Soul Asylum, the Jayhawks, and the Replacements, offers us a contract. The receptionist, Roz, answers the phone with this sexy, throaty voice. "Twin/Tone Records," she purrs. She makes the place seem bona fide even though their checks sometimes bounce.

We share a practice space with Soul Asylum in the back of the Twin/Tone building, reached through a door in the alley down the block from Joe's Chicken Shack. A room full of empty beer bottles, cigarette butts, and old set lists. Their bassist, Karl, saves me all his GHS Bassics strings from their tours because he changes them every single show. I have a whole shoebox full.

We head to Seattle to record our first album with Jack Endino, the guy who produced Nirvana and Mudhoney for Sub Pop. Seattle is an ideal place to work because of the melancholic atmosphere and killer coffee. Reciprocal Recording is in a little brick triangular building on a corner in a residential neighborhood. The studio is a small dark cave; Jack with his headphones on, the reel-to-reel tapes rolling, the lights on the engineering board, the darkness of the room, unable to differentiate between day and night. We record the album in five days with the tiniest budget, playing the tracks live, the three of us again setting up our equipment in one open room and getting it down in a couple of takes. Where there are little mistakes, like when I am a little off on the last note of "He's My Thing," we leave them in.

"We don't need to be all perfect," we say.

Kat stays late to help with the mixing. I understand why she likes being there late at night—it's a universe all its own—but Lori and I leave to hang out with our local friends because we think the studio is kind of boring.

Lori comes up with the title of the album, *Spanking Machine*, a game from her childhood where a birthday boy or girl crawls through a tunnel of people who spank them as a weird way to celebrate. The name Babes in Toyland is also from Lori's youth, one of her favorite movies as a kid.

Dan Corrigan, Minneapolis's most famous rock photographer, shoots the record cover. We go thrifting for toys and dolls and borrow more from everyone we know. We lie in a big pile of them for our cover shot. I wear a pair of stretchy, spotted cow-print pants, a fashion choice that I will grow to regret. "Remember those cow pants?" my bandmates like to ask me, getting a big sarcastic hardy-har every single time.

*Our first record, **Spanking Machine**, released in 1990*

THE MEAT TRUCK

We make our first video, for the song "He's My Thing." Because of our limited budget, the director, Phil Harder, can rent the camera for only a day, recording live scenes at 7th Street Entry and animated sequences using 16mm film. We go to Lowry Hill Liquors after we get the live shots, then back to Big Trouble House to watch them work.

Wooden posts, syringes, random tools and bolts, and old toys lie on the basement floor. There is a scary doll with big eyes that someone gave to the band, but we can't remember who; it's the same one with matted blonde hair that appears on *Spanking Machine.* In the video, Big Eye has a He-Thing doll boyfriend, scrawny and creepy, wearing a black cloak. She keeps him frozen for a while, but decides to thaw him so they can hang out. She pulls him out of the freezer. Later Big Eye catches He-Thing with another doll, a spooky old baby doll with crazy teeth and a blue dress. He crafts a music box ballerina and gives it to Crazy Teeth as a gift. She plays with it, enthralled. Big Eye sees this happen and then cuts off Crazy Teeth's leg. She brings it to He-Thing as an offering. He is pissed! He breathes fire on Big Eye and melts off her face.

The End.

The animator, Mike Etoll, uses a trick that simulates true animation by moving the dolls in real time while Phil quickly snaps the frames. The result is a crude version of stop-motion. In one shot, two hypodermic needles are stuck

A few of the dolls from the video for "He's My Thing"

in the main doll's head; Mike uses them to turn her live-action instead of shooting frame-by-frame. The first piece they animate is a vintage Tonka truck that passes through one of the scenes. The crew rolls up some ham and puts it in the back of the vehicle, which we dub The Meat Truck.

When the music box ballerina melts before they capture a clear shot, Mike makes another one out of clay.

UNFAMILIAR HAND

We're on tour again. Just the three of us this time, in San Francisco. I'm in the Mission District, getting a burrito at La Cumbre.

I order a shrimp burrito, the most expensive item on the menu, with extra sour cream and guacamole, grilled green onions, and a strawberry soda. This meal costs $9, which is a huge splurge, but I don't care. I broke down and asked my parents to send $50 so I wouldn't have to eat smoked oysters on all our days off. They sent $100. I do not tell Lori or Kat about my fat stack of cash.

I stare at the prawns as they sizzle in front of me.

The lady at the counter is getting my drink when everything starts shaking, light fixtures swinging and clanging, bottles and cans falling off the shelf behind the counter, breaking glass chattering like chimes. Confusion becomes fear, voices rise and build into panic. People scatter like pigeons.

They all head out the door. I follow.

Kat is on the beach, with a boy. They see the ocean surging and think the world is ending.

Lori is at a friend's house, still asleep. The quake throws her out of bed. She thinks a war has started.

I am on the street, the ground snakes and comes alive, a force pushing from below, emerging, creating a gash.

The old man next to me is alone, too, and we clutch each other, holding his unfamiliar hand, the texture of his shirt as I pull on it. We hang on to each other while the earth breaks open.

It's October 17, 1989. This earthquake will be best known for interrupting the World Series. I never get my food.

I walk back to the house and find Lori. We go out into the streets. All around is chaos, buildings on fire, broken glass scattered like jewels. Storefronts wide open and vulnerable suddenly have a different meaning. Houses are severed from their foundations, crumbled like matchsticks and cardboard.

People, gentle and stunned. Storekeepers with flashlights let customers in one by one for supplies. Later we hang out with strangers on a rooftop. They lend us instruments and we all play music together. The scene is nihilistic but not violent. Connection and lost boundaries.

In this landscape, no one is alone.

SUPERSTITION FREEWAY

Back on the road, we're traveling through the Arizona desert. The tour is fluid, we are perennials, riding in the new van we bought before we left home, a former military vehicle, forest green. We love Army Van: $2500, well maintained, low miles, still no backseats like Vanna, but much bigger. And no fucked-up clutch; Vanna shifted oddly, and Lori and I were the only ones who had mastered the finding-the-gear trick.

Army Van moves smoothly, without tricks. The new loft is just the right height.

It's hot, the scenery is burnt, amber and cinnamon, moss-colored cactus, cornflower sky. We don't have AC, the windows are open. The air is fever, phosphorescent, creeping across your skin. The drifting terrain watches us as we pass.

Kat is in The Princess Seat, wearing dark sunglasses, a red lace dress, short white socks, boy's black military shoes. She ties a wide ribbon in her hair, glances at herself in the rearview mirror, sips some water, pages through a magazine. She gets all the attention. In photos and videos, Lori and I are shadows. We try to ignore this, but sometimes it's hard.

Lori drives. I sit on the floor in the back, trying to read, but I'm too nauseated. I stare at Lori's dreads for a while, trying to see what's all the way in there, until I see her eyes in the rearview mirror as she catches me.

Kat and Lori, right before the accident in Arizona, 1989

I climb into the loft. The sound of the tires on the road pacifies my body and mind, familiar and rhythmic. I sink into the deep sleep of heat and boredom.

There's a piercing crash, a sharp jolt and sudden stop. I fly out of the loft and land on the floor. By the time I realize where I am, Lori has pulled over. A cop appears, almost immediately, out of the shimmering desert. He looks like Eric Estrada. Lori is freaked out, but not hurt. Kat is flecked with blood, face and legs embedded with glass. There is no other car. Nothing visible we hit. We are standing on the side of the highway, cars and trucks speeding past, faces through windows glancing at the scene. The roof of Army Van is peeled back like our oyster tins, the windshield on the Princess side shattered, shards everywhere.

Lori is talking to the cop, and there is a lady officer, too, writing notes on a pad, helping Kat, who remains calm. She goes to the hospital in an ambulance.

When the moment settles, I ask Lori what happened. A pickup truck driving the other direction lost its tire, which gathered momentum in the gully between the east- and westbound lanes of U.S. Route 60, known as Superstition Freeway. The tire flew into the air, crashed through the passenger-side windshield, bounced off, and faded into the desert.

A picture of Kat sitting in the cop car becomes the cover of our new single, "House." On the back cover is a young Lori, also bleeding, her nose bashed by her then-boyfriend.

We buy the Peanut Butter Cup, a brown two-toned Ford Econoline with real backseats, from a car rental place in Phoenix. The seller tells us the vehicle was owned by a woman who was kidnapped and is currently missing. He gives us a good deal.

Record cover with photo of Kat after the accident; on the flip side, a young Lori after being punched in the nose by a boyfriend

GIRLFRIENDS

I feel so hopeful as the signs on the highway start counting down the miles 'til we reach Minneapolis. I finally have my own apartment and love being there alone.

Girlfriends. All my best girlfriends are at home. We do normal things like going out to lunch, or thrift shopping for glass grapes and '50s chalkware fish, or to the movies, or walking around the lakes. Hanging out at the bookstore in Uptown buying magazines and new books that we trade when we are done reading them. Bike rides and long talks over coffee.

I tell my friends how sick I am of Lori and Kat.

Eva, Anne, me, and Maya at my apartment in Minneapolis

TUFFY

It's the middle of winter. The air so sharp and cold it hurts to breathe. Snow falling from the sky. As cars pass, all the kids on your block stare down the busy road waiting for the yellow school bus to arrive at the end of Hobby Oak Drive. Everyone standing in front of the sign where the letters of your street name are mounted; the D missing because your sister, Denise, took it and put it on her bedroom door.

You're in second grade, wearing the red snowmobile suit with flowered trim that your mom won in the raffle at a children's clothing store in downtown Hopkins, writing her name on a slip of paper and putting it in a jar. "I've never won anything before," she said, thrilled. But you hate your snowsuit. That's what babies wear! You want a ski jacket.

Out in the cold, you think about how badly you want a dog, one like Tuffy, the shaggy brown mutt who once belonged to a kid on your block. Tuffy, who came to the bus stop in the mornings as you all waited, licking and wagging his tail, hanging out with his boy, Jeremy, who's in the same grade as you. At the beginning of the school year, you were all petting Tuffy when he saw a squirrel and ran into the road. The car tried to stop but couldn't, squealing tires and black marks on the road that lasted for days. Tuffy yelped loudly, then he was quiet and lying in the middle of the road.

The woman got out of her car and started crying. Jeremy ran home, bawling and yelling for his mom. Just after he left, the bus pulled up down the road, away from the accident. The rest of you didn't know what to do, so you got on the bus and left.

Jeremy stayed home from school that day; normally you'd be jealous of that. The next day, no one knew what to say to him, so you didn't say anything at all, which made you feel even worse.

BABIES

We're on our first European tour promoting *Spanking Machine*, performing in England, Scotland, the Netherlands, Belgium, and Germany. Spending a day off in Berlin going to flea markets, out for long walks. We film a segment for a TV show where they ask us to sit in a playpen full of toys.

"Grown women don't sit in playpens," we say. Not comprehending, the film crew, very proud of their idea, keep pointing at the baby area, saying words we can't understand, nodding, smiling.

"We're not going to sit in there," three heads vigorously shaking NO.

Babes translates to *babies* in German, causing confusion. "We aren't fucking babies!" yells Kat, loud and scary, motioning to Lori and me, the playpen. They bring over some chairs.

"What's it like to be girls in a band?" the host asks.

That evening, everyone starts gathering in the streets. They tell us that the Berlin Wall is coming down, signifying the downfall of communism in East Berlin. They already stopped regulating the border. Only a year before, people trying to escape the East were being shot by soldiers guarding the border.

The scene becomes fully energized as the crowd grows bigger.

The twelve-foot-high wall is made of concrete slabs and is covered with vibrant graffiti. People use whatever they can find to break off pieces: hammers, metal stakes, rocks. Lori takes a chunk. Eventually, there is a hole big enough for us to climb through, so Lori, Kat, and I cross into East Berlin, where there are celebrations everywhere, cars honking, people drinking and smoking, grownups dancing like children. Bonfires glow and sparklers flicker in the air. Cameras flash like lightning. Folks simultaneously laughing and crying, helping each other get over the wall to the other side. In another part of town soldiers are spraying crowds with big hoses, telling them to get down, but where we are, the teenage guards have soft wheat hair, their uniforms the dark green of avocado peels, neatly pressed, caps sharply creased. They smile. Fine young ladies have their pictures taken with the soldiers, embracing them, luminous, lit by the moon.

Spun

I live inside
All invited inside
Eyes flutter feathers
My hair's fair like weather
I've blown my recovery
Living is nice
When you're spun like a kite

EXTRA LONELY

I have no idea why we're asked to open for Skinny Puppy on their Too Dark Park tour. They're a scary industrial band with a huge cult following. But it pays pretty well, so we can afford to have Howard along. I put a silver glitter pickguard on the new black Fender Jazz Bass I bought after my P-Bass got stolen from our van the last time we were in New York.

During the Skinny Puppy concert, numerous video screens show different graphically violent videos: actual footage of a man committing suicide by shooting himself in the head; a Japanese snuff film of a guy dismembering a girl that is maybe/maybe not real; footage of animal vivisection. Their singer, Ogre, comes on stage with his head wrapped in a bandage, just his nose showing, and sits in this tree sculpture with limbs that hold fake syringes, the main part of their set. A man in a Jason mask comes out periodically to attack him. There is a shit-ton of fake blood spurting *all the time*. One night Ogre puts his finger down his throat and pukes on stage.

They have a big tour bus and sometimes Kat rides along, but Lori and I do not get invited. Kat's been making out with Ogre, but since they both are involved with other people they made a rule of only going up the shirt, she tells me. I consider making out with the drummer so I can ride on the bus too but decide that's a bad idea.

I do not understand the crowd that comes to see Skinny Puppy. There seems to be a lot of drugs and black clothes and dudes that are extra lonely. One thing I do know, they do not like Babes in Toyland, as evidenced by the shouts of "You suck!" and "Get off the stage!"

Mostly I hang out in our dressing room during Skinny Puppy's shows. Occasionally I watch from the side of the stage and try really hard to not look at the movies, although sometimes I peek and regret it. I get so freaked out that, when I hear their music start, I have to leave. But one night Howard and I decide to really check out the show. When Ogre slips on fake blood and falls on his ass, we do not stop cracking up for days.

Howard and me, Minneapolis

EVERYONE

People recognize me out at shows, or shopping for groceries, at the movies, in line at the post office. Everyone acts extra friendly, buying drinks and introducing themselves. I am not sure who is for real, if someone is really interested in knowing me or just wanting in on the scene. All this attention gives me a false sense of self-worth, illusive and distorted, with the ability to vanish like melting snow. I define myself through the gaze of strangers and I have never felt so phony. I have never felt so whole. I am disconnected, capable of caring very little, especially about those who are the closest to me. I am losing myself but it doesn't matter. Boys think I'm foxy and want to make out. Girls want to be my friend; they also try to make out with me. Everyone thinks I'm really great.

My apartment in Minneapolis

JUST ANOTHER PUNK BAND

Sonic Youth are most everybody's favorite band—punk and experimental, feedback and noise, immaculate discord. Their music offers an entrance to a profound emotional place found in chaos. When we are asked to open for them on their European tour for the album *Goo*, we go kabonkers.

When a writer asks their guitar player, Thurston, about us and some of the other female bands like L7 and Hole, he coins the term *foxcore*, because he says dopey things like that. Now we get foxcore questions everywhere we go, as if it's a real thing.

We do an interview with Everett True, a famous music journalist in England, for the magazine *NME*. They take pictures of us in a London flea market, sheer white dresses hanging behind us on a clothesline as we sit on the ground. Everett asks a riveting question: "What's it like to be girls in a band?" Lori kids that we get our periods at the same time. I cringe. Kat then talks about her stepmother beating her for not doing her chores properly. Lori mentions a guy whipping his dick out at her. "Is there anything else you would like to know?" I ask.

The interview questions I like best are the ones that explore our personalities, like "What's your favorite holiday?" or "What's your favorite food?" College fanzine writers are often great that way, like their intentions are pure, wanting to know more about you. Those interviews are actually fun.

But now on this tour, journalists keep asking us if we are "riot girls." We don't really know what that means or if it's supposed to be *grrrl* or *girl*, but we figure it's another stupid thing like foxcore or grunge, so we say, "No." These same writers want to know what our parents think of our being in a band, a question they never ask boys.

I find out that riot grrrl is a movement all about feminism and politics and activism, with music and writing as a focus. I think what the riot grrrl bands are doing is really important and excellent, but we aren't all smart and motivated like that. We're just another punk band, like our friends the Cows.

But we don't mind being called "underground," because that sounds like we live in a secret world, which is true.

A STRANGE HABITAT

Things start out awkwardly when we end up traveling on Sonic Youth's tour bus instead of in our own van when the tour begins. They are surprised that we don't have our own vehicle; we are puzzled too. It's like someone totally cheaped out, but we're not sure who. The situation never gets resolved, and we end up riding with them for the entire tour.

As we travel across Europe, we live in a strange habitat. I sleep in my top bunk as we pass through England and the Netherlands and Germany and Italy. Waking up in the next town and living nearly the same day again.

Caterers travel with us and prepare all our meals, so we never have to worry about food. I spend the day watching the crew set up, reading books in quiet corners. Interviews and soundchecks, waiting to perform. Many of the shows are outdoors, in the middle of fields out in the country, nowhere to go outside of the venue. We play daily to giant crowds who really dig us, everyone going mental up front—dancing, slamming, stage diving, singing along to all the words. Signing records and t-shirts and posters, again and again. Talking to the fans after the concert, every night women hug us and tell us that they are starting a band because we inspired them. I find these outpourings touching and sweet. I would like to consider myself an inspiration, especially to other women, but these moments of success are soaked in a loneliness that I cannot understand.

Listening to Sonic Youth from the side of the stage: "Schizophrenia" and "Kool Thing" and "Tunic (Song for Karen)"—the haunting lyrics, "I feel like I'm disappearing, getting smaller every day." These songs become permanent triggers in my brain that return me to this bittersweet place in time.

Sonic Youth's had the same crew forever, and I hang out with them more than I do the musicians, spending time with the roadies, soundmen, and techs. Lori is always the center of attention with her volume and energy. She's an explorer, finding the record shop, museum, or antique store even when we are out in the middle of nowhere. I get jealous when she returns with amazing new purchases or stories, but I know it's my own fault for being too lazy to go along.

Kat sleeps off her hangovers during the day, emerging more beautiful than ever. No one understands how she does it, and still in that same black velvet dress.

Sonic Youth's bassist, Kim, is kind and sincere, but also intimidating. I always trip and fall or do something else embarrassing when she is around. Blushing when I talk to her. But even though they are Sonic Youth, they are pretty normal people. Thurston is really friendly and funny. Lee, the other guitarist, always seems to be thinking and really listens when you talk. Steve, the drummer, goes to bed even earlier than I do. I never see any of them get wasted.

But I get pretty homesick. One thing that is never OK to say on a rock tour is "I miss my mom."

One night, Kat gets drunk and storms into Sonic Youth's dressing room when we're all hanging out. It's after the show, yet really early. She kicks a coffee table filled with lit candles and wine glasses, knocking everything over. She spits on the floor. It's understood that it's my job to take her away.

"Do you want to go to bed," I say, the way you ask a toddler.

"Yes," she nods.

Hooking arms like grannies and taking her back to her bunk, I put her under the blankets like she is my child.

Concert pass, Paris, 1990

TEA AND TOAST

Shopping at the grocery store is one of our favorite parts of being in England; all the different kinds of biscuits and canned fish and sauces and jams, the way everything is slightly different. We come home to our rented brick flat in the Wood Green district of London, the place we're staying while recording our second album with John Loder as producer. He is known for being a groundbreaker in exposing new music. He runs both Southern Records, which distributes Twin/Tone and other indie labels in the U.K., and Southern Studios out of the garage of his house. Again we record the tracks live, but with additional overdubs of guitar and vocals. It requires several takes to make sure all the songs are tight. His wife makes us tea and toast when we take breaks, hanging out in their kitchen.

Shortly after we arrive, Kat finds out that her birth mother died of pancreatic cancer. She doesn't cry, at least not in front of us, saying she already did that. She stays in her room and writes. We decide to call the album *To Mother*, a childhood photograph of her mom, Lynne, on the cover, a picture of each of us as a child on the back.

Kat and John Loder, London, 1990

BOOBS IN BUTTLAND

We still get asked about our gender in almost every interview. People want to know. I like to say that I don't care, but the fact that I get irritated at the questions must mean I give at least a few fucks. I wonder how to separate when the question is sexist from when the writer is unoriginal. Both get on our nerves. I shut down and get quiet. I'm not saying gender doesn't make a difference, I just don't know how to articulate the difference in a way that makes other people feel satisfied.

Maybe I'm too wide-eyed, but being treated differently by soundmen or club owners, a common complaint of touring women, actually seems more dependent on the status of our band than on our gender. The more success we achieve, the less condescension and the fewer assumptions about our incompetence, real or perceived, we experience. Plenty of boys complain about the house soundmen being dicks too. Maybe that's just a crabby guy's job. But for the dudes, ability doesn't reflect any larger than the musical realm; for women the judgment is all-encompassing.

You can be a feminist and have a man help you carry a heavy-as-fuck amp. You can work a crappy office job, wear grocery store pantyhose, and still be a member of NOW. You can sport baby barrettes and velvet mini-dresses with big collars from the '60s, and that does not make you a "kinderwhore," a term some dumbshit coined. Whore?

Areyoukiddingme? I see Wednesday Addams, sinister and all-knowing.

Women musicians can wear whatever they want. They can be virtuosos or hardly know how to play at all. They can be all kinds of things, experience all emotions, everything, all the time, all at once.

Babes in Toyland don't need to talk girl-power to the press; we are living it. Watch us, ladies. Start your own band. Do whatever you love.

The writers call us Babe-ra-ham Lincolns, Babes Ruthless, Babes in the Woods. They use stupid headlines like "Spanks for the Memories." I don't care. Call us Boobs in Buttland if you want. Just realize that Kat will throw a bottle at your sorry self if you piss her off. She will. She'll aim for your head. And I'll be standing right there behind her.

THE MOTORCYCLE TRAILS

An old lady teacher at your junior high says she saw you smoking pot as you waited at the bus stop on Hobby Oak Drive. You have never smoked pot in your life, but she says she saw you there by the sign as she drove by in her car during a snowstorm. She says she could see you were puffing on marijuana and not a cigarette (which you have never smoked either) by the way you inhaled. You tell the principal you were probably warming your hands. Still, they call your mom and tell her to look through your bedroom, and you are so mad when she does, and, ha!—nothing to see. They search your locker right in the middle of passing time when all the kids are looking, and, ha!—nothing to see. Now everyone thinks you're the stoner girl of eighth grade, but you like it when the Pink Floyd boys start calling your house.

Summer is almost over. The milkweed plants going to seed, silvery-white ghosts rise into the sky. The rusty sumac berries like pomegranate seeds, tall wheaty grass scratching your bare legs.

There are hardly any punker or new wave boys at your school, so the next best thing is those Pink Floyd stoners: long hair, hint of a mustache, line from a chew tin worn into the back pockets of their Levi's. Hanging out with your friend Serena and three stoner boys. No one was home at your house so you take a mason jar, add a little booze from each bottle in your parents' liquor cabinet, and walk to the

Me with mullet, eighth grade class picture

motorcycle trails—the nearby woods where people dump old bedsprings and race dirt bikes.

You wear cut-offs and a t-shirt from the Devo concert you went to for your birthday, covering boobs that will grow from an A cup to a C cup this year. The sun's going down. Flaming light beams across the horizon and everything looks bittersweet and golden. You hear grasshoppers jumping, birds, the wind. Everything smelling clean like rain and mud puddles. You can identify most of the bugs because this is where you collected them for your science project, pinning them on a board, labeling the names. Lepidoptera, Diptera, Coleoptera. You spot a walking stick on a leaf.

Serena is with the best guy because she is prettier and more experienced than you. They vanish into the trees.

You are left with the other two guys as the spirits in the jar make you feel warm and giggly, although you are timid. One of the boys kisses you as the other stands there watching. Putting his stiff tongue in your mouth, sloppy, touching your breasts outside of your shirt. The boys whisper to each other and then start grabbing you, pulling on your Devo shirt, trying to take it off. They stretch it all out. You kick and slap, spilling the jar and running all the way home.

You are one of the fastest girls on the track team at school.

The stoner who kissed you shows up at your house shortly after that, politely ringing the doorbell, standing under the eave where a bird built her nest, the mother bird squawking protectively at his approach.

"I bet you would have liked that if we were alone in the woods," he says when you answer the door.

You feel so little when you tell him, "yes."

WOLF OR BEAR

I meet Joe Cole at a show we play in Hollywood. He is nine years older and a foot taller. I can't believe this kind of a boy is interested in me: from California, famous close friends like Kim, Thurston, and Henry Rollins. Long thick hair, eyelashes looking like he just got out of the shower, separate, the kind a girl is supposed to have. His body is soft and lean, big like a wolf or a bear, whichever one is never supposed to be alone.

Joe wants to talk to me after the set but is too afraid, so he just says "Hi" and "I liked the show," and he feels like a dumbass because of that.

But I remember him.

"I thought you might not be able to speak English. You look like some little Spaniard or Italian lady," he also says.

I like being mistaken for an immigrant girl just off the boat.

My hair's grown out from the pixie cut on our first album cover. I'm skinnier and have cheekbones now. Recently the photographers have moved me from the side or background of the band photos to the middle.

Courtney Love, who is not that well known yet, is another friend of Joe's. He sometimes roadies for Hole, the same job he used to have for Black Flag, Henry Rollins's former band. We stay with Courtney when we return to California later that year. She is always nice to me. That night after we play, Courtney tells me that I have to hang

Portrait of Joe

out with Joe. "He really likes you. Go talk to him," she says
and pushes me into him, like junior high.

He lives in Venice Beach in a studio apartment painted
Easter-egg pastels. His bed is a futon on a makeshift loft
like a shelf, right below a window facing the alley. There's
a guy who lives out there; we can see him as we wake up
the next morning, my head on Joe's chest. Unable to really

make out because Lori is sleeping on the floor below us, even though we tried to ditch her.

There is something honey-kissed about this boy. He smells like the sun.

Joe shows me his photographs, mostly black and white, lovely: someone who has fallen down on the street, a homeless vet looking straight into the camera.

He tells me it's hard for him to be happy. I know what he means.

We eat pancakes at an outdoor café before I leave that afternoon. That night, I ride in the van loft listening to The Pixies' *Surfer Rosa* loud on my Walkman, feeling super fine. When we arrive at a club in Chicago a few days later, I find out that Joe called and left the manager his number for me.

"I was jonesing to talk to you."

That's what he says when I call him back, crouched in the stairwell of the warehouse where we're staying, twirling the spiral phone cord around my hand, plugging one ear so I can hear. We talk for an hour. We start to talk every night. Then every day and every night. He understands my life, the monotony and boredom, why you might make out with a stranger when you are wasted.

I return to Minneapolis a few weeks later, my small place with hardwood floors, a vintage stove and fridge, everything painted white. In the mail comes a large envelope with a finger painting in primary colors, two stick figures holding hands. He'd painted "I love you" on the back, sitting on the floor of his place, long legs crisscrossed like a little boy. The clean hair falling into his face smells of heather and thyme.

Mad Pilot

You are the one that feels like no one's home
To be left alone is like the marrow from my bones
You are the one
You are the one

DAISIES IN A WINE BOTTLE

The boys I sleep with in Minneapolis build beer-can pyramids. Joe, however, shops at the co-op, which is rare for a guy. He hardly drinks.

"Why are you always drunk?"

"I'm twenty-one. I'm supposed to be drunk. You are so mean," I say, drunk.

There are so many things he wants, projects and plans that he feels are failing.

"I feel like I am cursed," he says.

People don't discuss depression much.

Phone booths in random towns, we talk. I become claustrophobic, burned out, alone. Kat, Lori, and I aren't getting along. The issues are always the same: how to spend our money; who is doing the most/least work of carrying gear, selling shirts, or driving the van; who is not giving full attention to the music.

He calms me down.

"I have to get out of here," I say quite often, meaning it.

He's the only one I can admit this to, feeling like an asshole complaining while we are successful. We talk about me quitting the band, moving into his little place. I am a girl with faith that a garden and a dog are all I need to be happy.

"Maybe I can work at the co-op," I say.

I get jealous when Joe shows me the Sonic Youth video for the song "My Friend Goo." I see him dancing with Kim. He seems to like that I'm possessive and insecure.

I love Joe

We fight a lot. We break up.

"There is just no way this can work," I say.

Then we continue talking on the phone and making plans like nothing happened.

"When am I going to see you?"

He can be so mean.

"Why would you ask me something so dumb?"

But mostly sweet.

"You're an angel who came to earth to show me how to be human."

In my daydreams, I come home and put daisies in a wine bottle, paint the walls jeweled colors, a bandana tied around my head, a pot of lentils on the stove. He hugs me, lifting me off the ground, my head nestled into his neck. We cling to each other tightly as the wannabe actresses of Venice Beach rollerblade past the door.

GHOSTS

On the roof of the apartment building in Venice Beach where Jim Morrison was said to have lived, Joe and I are lying on a blanket, listening to the ocean, looking at the sky, talking. It's the week of my twenty-second birthday.

We have breakfast at the farmers market in L.A. with Kim and Thurston. I can't believe this is my life. People recognize them and I imagine they wonder why I'm there. I meet a bunch of Joe's friends, including Dave Markey, a filmmaker who has featured Joe in several of his movies. Joe and Dave think it's dorky that I want to see a *Wheel of Fortune* taping for my birthday, but they go along with the plan. Joe grew up in L.A.; his dad was a soap opera actor who was once married to Jaclyn Smith from *Charlie's Angels*. His father taped the show *The Young and the Restless* in the same studio as *Wheel of Fortune*, and Joe worked there as an extra too. It was my second-favorite show when I was a kid; we'd have to get up way too early to be in the audience for my #1 show, *The Price Is Right*.

I also meet his best friend, Henry Rollins, who is kind, straightforward, self-assured. I make them pasta for dinner. Joe says Henry thinks I'm smart because I know how to cook, but I don't feel smart. I feel like I am somewhere I don't belong.

The next day, Joe and I take mushrooms. He is mostly clean but OK with those drugs because they're natural, he says. We have lunch at Canter's Deli. I go to the bathroom, and a skinny, boozed-up lady with frizzy hair stumbles out of the stall while still pulling up her pants. I see her unruly bush just as the mushrooms kick in. She fumbles back into the Kibutz Room, the bar attached to the restaurant. When I get back to the table, the chicken I ordered has arrived, but looks way too grotesque to eat, my mind wiggling, thinking the pieces will start moving around and squawking like in the movie *Eraserhead*.

We can't stop talking about squawking chickens or the pubic hair lady, worried she's following us, wanting to show her bush again, maybe even trying to touch it to our skin. We stop at a vintage clothing store. I know he can't afford that '70s flowered mini, but I am super happy when he buys it for me anyway. I put it on in the dressing room and wear it out the door. We later walk on the beach and he keeps grabbing my legs, making me fall, which was funny at first, but after a while I get mad, then he still does it a few more times.

Joe carries a picture of me in his wallet, black and white. I'm about one year old. In the photo, I've fallen, sitting on the ground, crying, looking at my hand like I scraped it. I re-create the pose for him on the beach, and we think this is comedy gold. Wandering around all afternoon long, still high. Happy. We think no one else can see us, so we call ourselves ghosts.

HONEY AND PROMISE

Grass turning from dry russet to lush green, feeling it between your toes as you walk barefoot across the lawn. The robins in high branches sing *cheep cheep cheep* like a Disney movie. The cherry trees with pink blossoms that bloom the earliest in spring, petals floating to the ground like a daydream. Tulips emerge after huddling all winter long. Lilacs that smell like honey and promise.

The last day of seventh grade. Everyone throws their papers into the garbage or up in the air, yelling "HOORAY!" as the bell finally rings.

You and your dad on a Sunday afternoon working in the backyard together, digging in the dirt, planting your garden like you do every year. Making little rows and placing the seeds, measuring with a yardstick that you got at the state fair to make sure they're not too close together. Planting tomatoes, cucumbers, squash, and sunflowers. Putting the seed packets on sticks so you'll know where everything will sprout. A scarecrow to daunt the rabbits and the squirrels. By this time next year you won't want to help your dad in the garden anymore, but today you drag the green garden hose over from the side of the house, taking a sip before giving the seeds a drink.

NEITHER HERE NOR THERE

The plane is dark and quiet in the deep hours of night, just the glow of the no-smoking signs and the hum of the engines. The movie ended an hour ago. A few people shuffle down the aisle to the bathroom or read by overhead light, but most try to find a way to get comfortable and fall asleep. I am envious of Lori and Kat, slumbering on either side of me. I can't drift off.

The pilot with his calm voice over the loudspeaker as we cross the ocean makes me feel lonely. Our cruising altitude. What we'll see if we look to our left or our right. I ask the flight attendant for another bottle of wine and then doze with my head on Lori's shoulder, but only for a moment. I wake up and think of him.

Hot towels and orange juice before landing at Heathrow. Making our way through the long lines at customs in the airless room filled with splotchy people in a wash of gray light. Everyone with the same status: neither here nor there.

We get to the front of the line and explain to the humorless staff why we are in the country, showing them our passports and visas, telling them about the band. They are skeptical but let us through. We wait for our luggage and guitars in baggage claim. The *thunk* of my bass as it lands on the carousel and makes its way around to where I can grab it, unsuccessfully trying not to hit anyone as I yank it off the moving ride. Our stuff fills up two shaky luggage carts that we push through the crowd, making our way outside to wait for John from Southern Records to pick us up. He tells us our album's doing well.

Record signing in Manchester, England, 1991

MILLIONAIRES

In Yugoslavia, when we get our $15 per diem, we are rich. We eat giant prawns with long antennae and eyeballs like currants, order fancy bottles of wine. We go to the city's shopping district, but there isn't anything we want to buy, only medical-looking footwear, orange lipstick, bags of dry biscuits. We try to spend all our money because it can't be exchanged outside the country, but that seems impossible. The cash we get each day has six zeros on the bills, so we call ourselves millionaires, eat more shellfish, and purchase fancy bottles of liqueurs to take home.

We play at Ljubljana Castle, on an open-air stage made of ancient stone like Greek ruins, beset by matching old buildings. It is my most beloved show of all.

Before the concert, the promoter takes us to the main castle: dark and velvety red inside, rustic chandeliers, long wooden tables, antlers on the walls, candles. We are served meat with an unrecognizable flavor and texture.

All the buildings match—chalky white walls, clay roof tiles. Ljubljana is like a storybook land, with winding canals, rolling hills, baroque statues, gray steeples. We stay at the stunning Grand Hotel, its ornate art deco detailing on the exterior, climbing fuchsia bougainvillea. Sharing one room with three very comfortable beds.

The breeze is warm, moist, and smelling of jasmine. The crowd is so happy to have us there. After the show, girls say, "Thank you, thank you, you are beautiful." They kiss our hands.

Boys, sexy boys who are young and tall with high cheekbones, lead us away, speaking the barest of English. We climb over fences to swim in pools wearing only our scanties. They take us to a dance club in the middle of a field. It's like an underground fallout shelter, steps down below the earth. We dance for hours. Later, fireworks sparkle in the sky. Everywhere we go, people are rejoicing. The boys tell us their country is celebrating its independence. We think they mean this is their version of the Fourth of July.

We wake up in our three comfortable beds. We go outside and see tanks rolling down the street, bigger than I ever imagined. Soldiers are everywhere. We are supposed to leave through Austria, but find out the border has been bombed. Our tour manager, Dino, explains that Slovenia and Croatia declared their independence from the rest of Yugoslavia that night. A war has begun as forces try to keep the country intact. We have to show our passports over and over again.

After Dino makes many serious phone calls, we drive nine hours to Hungary to exit the country. There are farmers, old sun-baked men, women with scarves wrapped around their heads, using simple tools to tend fields. As we pass, they make motions with their hands, like shooting machine guns, warning us of what might be up ahead.

We stop at a small store in a remote rural area. The biggest pig we've ever seen stands next to the building behind a fence, pink and apathetic. Lori and I wave and oink as a greeting. The shopkeepers, a husband and wife, are happy to have us there. The shop is sparsely stocked. They show us where the orange soda is, excited, because that's what Americans want. Taking the orange soda, we hug them before we leave, giving them all our remaining Yugoslavian money. They can't speak English, but make motions with their hands, like shooting machine guns.

We wait in a long line of cars, terrified by the time we reach the border. At the small brick building just ahead, people are getting turned away.

Dino digs around in the van and finds a magazine. He talks to the guards, trying to explain why we are there. They don't understand. He points to our picture on one of the pages, then at the three girls sitting together in the backseat. They come up to the window and ask if we play like AC/DC.

They love AC/DC.

"Yes!"

The guards want their photos taken with us. We sign lots of records, posters, and t-shirts.

After we cross, it takes several hours to find someplace to stay. The cities in Hungary have really long names like Felsoszenterzsebet or Zalaegerszeg. We find a hotel, but the only place to sleep is in the sauna. We each stretch out on a bench.

JACKED

After the show in Amsterdam, a haze of cobblestone walkways, streetlights glowing amber and red, canals and arched bridges, buildings made of timeworn brick, girls on their bikes ringing the bells as they whir past.

There are cafés where we smoke, bars where I giggle when I spill my beer. The new friends we make lead us around, taking us through the alleys and back doors that open into the buzzing hive of each new club.

We're performing at a festival in rural France the next afternoon and need to leave in the middle of the night to arrive on time. My favorite new friend is a straw-haired young Dutchman. He wants to come along. "No boys in the van" is usually the rule, but all three of us like this fellow, who looks hot in his suit jacket. He's our new best friend.

"He's so funny!" we say to each other when he tells a bad joke. We make out in one of the alleys.

Dino tries to talk us out of bringing the boy along to France, but we three girls are sloppy, belligerent, not very nice.

"We are the bosses."

Our Europe van is fancy, with a TV/VCR combo. Our soundman, Stephan, drives a separate vehicle filled with gear. Dino drives the van, and we each get a cushy row, enough room to lie down. Kat in the middle covered by her furry coat. Lori in the front, staying awake, listening to music, bass sneaking out of the headphones. The pulse of the van traveling down the road. My new friend and I take the last row, downy blanket and pillows.

In the back, we drink vodka as he whispers what he wants to do to me. It's very dark in the van. He tells me my skin smells warm like an American beach, and he puts his hand up my dress.

"It smells like fucking in here!" Kat wakes up and announces. I pull away red with shame and fall into a mean vodka sleep.

Waking up with the morning rays. Luscious meadows full of sunflowers, heads turned away shyly as they laze in the sun. Out the window, the landscape rolls with yellow and green as far as I can see. We pass an exit leading to Orléans, the town where my parents lived when they were young, my dad stationed in the army.

The evening comes back to me. I look at the guy next to me, who is not that cute, his nails and pants dirty. His smile reveals teeth jacked. He keeps trying to hold my hand, sitting way too close. I can't stretch out; I need to throw up.

And something is very off with this one, something in his head. I soon find out that he doesn't have money to get back home.

We get to the outdoor festival site. I am able to avoid the boy most of the day, dissipating into the large crowd, harboring backstage.

After we play, I sneak back to the hotel, still drink-sick. The sun has just gone down. I try to eat something, take a long shower, fall asleep tucked cleanly into my bed.

There's a knock.

I tell him I'm sleeping, but the boy wants to come in. He wants to come in very badly, pounding on the door. He starts calling me "Fucking Bitch," saying he should have picked the blonde one. I stay quiet, but he won't stop clamoring.

I call the front desk and ask for Dino's room. The desk lady doesn't speak English, but we figure it out. I tell Dino what's happening.

Soon I hear rational voices outside the door, Dino, and Stephan, too, reasonable and assertive, telling him it's time to go. He can sleep on their floor, they say.

We are far from any city and know he can't come with us when we leave. I pace around my room, wanting to dematerialize, wanting to go home, wanting to see Joe. Everyone is mad at me. I hate myself most of all.

I give Dino my saved-up per diem when he comes to check on me. He gives it to the guy for the bus. Later, when I head out of my cave and into the van, there's that yelling again, "Fucking Bitch." But now everyone is mad at him instead of me.

He throws a rock at the van as we drive away. Misses.

Concert poster from our tour with Skunk, the Netherlands, 1991

Pearl

Off with their heads 'cause I'm staying in bed
Sick of the blackbird that shrieks in my head

A TINY SPECK

We play festivals all across Europe, rural spaces transformed as stages are built, backdrops hung, lights mounted, concession stands stocked.

I walk around before the crowds get there. The unique energy of expectation, the hum.

I walk around as the crowd leaves. The place deflated, post-apocalyptic with fields turned to mud from rain, trash everywhere. I like it quiet this way. Vendors packing up booths selling earrings or records or t-shirts tell me how much our band means to them. Someone snaps a photo, my arm around their friend. I sign dozens of autographs, never saying no. I identify with being a fan; what I can't fathom is what it means to be me right now.

At night, guitars are packed up in their velveteen-lined cases. Drum sets broken down into smaller pieces: stands and foot pedals, cymbals and kick drums and bass drums and snares, each in its own black case. Cords wound neatly before they are placed into gear bags, distortion pedals untaped from the stage, set lists thrown away. Backdrops rolled up, lights and stages taken down, everything loaded into trucks and vans. Musicians getting drunker and drunker.

Often we travel during the wee hours to the next town. There is nothing to talk about, there is no one to call, there's nothing to worry about. The hotel rooms are booked, our meals are arranged. Our equipment is loaded

With John Peel and his son at the Reading Festival, 1991

in and out for us. My bass is tuned, and the strings are changed. We have interviews scheduled all day, every day. The only other thing I have to do is perform music for an hour. I am always so excited for that moment to arrive.

The festivals bring thousands of fans. Security guys in front protect us. People passing out and getting carried off on stretchers. Walking through the dense audience is too claustrophobic, so I usually stay backstage. But I don't always hang out with the other bands the way Kat and Lori do. I don't want to get wasted; I'll feel like shit the next day. Catching a ride with whoever goes back to the hotel first.

Reading Festival is the biggest concert of all. On the bill with Sonic Youth, Dinosaur Jr., Nirvana, and Iggy Pop. Joe's in town working for Hole and has the day off to spend with me. We have several interviews after the show, so we don't get to watch many other bands. But Joe and I do get a chance to see Dinosaur Jr. Dave Markey is there, too, making a documentary about Sonic Youth. He films us as we dance. We meet John Peel, the man famous for discovering and promoting underground bands on his BBC radio show.

I am not nervous to perform even when I see that there are thousands of people who seem to go back for miles, not when Kat shows up only a half hour before our set, and not even when we go on and our amps won't turn on right away. Once we begin, I decide no one can see me because I can't see them. Believing myself invisible breaks me open, especially as the wind blows through me, as if it could lift me like a kite. I am just a tiny speck, photographed from the sky, part of a map that includes a large stage, a drum set and amps, Lori behind me, Kat to the right, and Joe standing over on my side of the stage, looking out for me.

Driving back to London, Joe and I tangle up together, are part of each other, falling asleep as we roll across the English countryside in the sweet quiet of the night.

Dust Cake Boy

Indian Billy simple sin scratches across my skin
Soft gravel scratches cross my skin
It ain't love, baby, that makes this martyr grin
Simply sick, where Billy's been

TIM CARR TAKES US TO MANNY'S

After we return from Europe, Kat and I are walking through the bar at the Green Mill restaurant on Hennepin Avenue in Minneapolis. Lori is on her way. We are meeting an A&R guy from Warner Brothers' Reprise label to discuss a recording deal. He accidentally saw one of our shows in New York at the Pyramid Club, going inside because it was raining. Even his sister is shocked that he wants to sign us because she thinks we suck, a common sentiment in Minneapolis and beyond.

As we scope the room, a guy at the bar is smiling devilishly at us, like *hey ladies.*

"Are you looking for me?" he says, with a big smile. We both say, "NO!" Gross.

He says, "No really, you are looking for me. I'm Tim Carr."

We each will get a $10,000 advance, so we sign. It's not like anyone else is making an offer.

Tim is actually charming, smart, cordial, and sincere. He really believes in us, even though screaming punk girls who are self-taught musicians aren't big chart busters. He is a huge supporter of little-known and, more importantly, unconventional bands. Tim is a local, also from Hopkins, and worked at the Walker Art Center in Minneapolis before moving to New York.

When Tim comes to town we go to the New French Cafe, the first small bistro with fancy-pants food in Minneapolis.

Kat, Lori, and I kick each other under the table and crack up as the server describes the specials in overwrought detail while making eye contact with us. We order *everything*.

Tim takes us to Manny's, which is a steakhouse where famous people, like basketball players and Andy Rooney, go when they come to town. A painting of a bull with giant testicles in the entryway, scotch and cigars. We sit in a booth in the bar and order big expensive lobsters. We put on bibs and chow down.

We soon return to Europe for a solo tour. Tim meets us in Paris with a playwright who is said to be quite famous, although we don't know who he is. They drive us around in the middle of the night after the show in a very tiny car, taking us to some secret swanky place at 2 a.m. with velvety curtains, white tablecloths, and ten pieces of silverware, each. We order *everything*. We tell the story and laugh about how we thought Tim was trying to hit on us at the Green Mill.

THE HALLOWEEN BLIZZARD

The other guys are more fun than Joe. Well, really, they aren't that fun—they are there. I drink enough to dissipate into a spiral-eyed world, and the boys then don't have to be that handsome, or smart, or nice to me. Gin & tonic–soaked nudity. Pale and meager rolling around. The sweet ones never get my notice for long.

When we were in London, Joe and I argued all the time. He was always in a bad mood and got on my nerves. One day we just did things separately; he went to the movies, and I headed to the museum to see the Cindy Sherman exhibit. I wonder if we'd be together if we lived in the same town.

Joe and me at my parents' house, 1991

The band takes a break after the European tour, coming home for a bit before returning to London to record in December. Joe visits Minneapolis and we get an epic blizzard on Halloween, twenty-six inches of snow. We are stuck at my place and watch movies, play Monopoly, and eat cereal like little kids. We bundle up and walk to the grocery store, come home and make french onion soup. It feels more like we are best friends than lovers, although we still are that too. He is the only person I can really talk to. Neither of us is very easy to understand.

We dig my purple Dodge Dart out of the snow, and I show him how to spin doughnuts in an empty parking lot. I have my hand on his leg as he drives. As I touch him, the distinct feeling that he is disappearing surges through me; Joe breaking down into fragments and diffusing into the air. When I tell him what I felt, he wasn't surprised. He had the same vision.

NOTE READERS

On our way to the BBC studios, John Loder shows us the spot where the Beatles crossed the road for the cover of *Abbey Road*. We are doing our second recording session for John Peel's radio show. Peel names *Spanking Machine* his favorite album of 1990. He asks me why I am always so quiet. "I want to be the mysterious one," I say. But more accurately, Lori and Kat hardly ever let me get a word in, so I have given up.

When Lori and I practice alone, there is no pressure to impress each other with our skills. We are both proud of and semi-oblivious to the fact that we don't know what the fuck we're doing—in a technical sense, that is. We look down on people (men) with "professional music skills," who "read the notes" and know "measures and time signatures" (*we're not writing a fucking waltz*), the same way we judge someone in a suit working in an office cubicle. There is egotism in creating our own thing, but also clarity, simple confidence that we *are* doing it right. Kat and Lori make me feel like a good bassist because my style is distinctive and self-created. They brag about it, in fact.

But the BBC studios are a different world. We record in separate rooms for the first time, each of us playing our instrument alone. The engineers are serious Englishmen, grownups, who work with really famous bands. They won't listen to us when we tell them we can't hear the bass or the kick drum enough, this passive-aggressive (or just plain

Kat and me with our friends in London: Sarah (bassist from the band Sun Carriage), Gary, and Andrew, 1991

aggressive) way of simply not doing what you ask, or just doing it the tiniest, stingiest bit imaginable, then acting like you are unreasonable for asking again, willing you to give up by being all British and indirect, not ever saying the truth: *We think you sound like shit.* But I come from a long line of women who keep asking for what they want, not worrying about being annoying.

"I still can't hear the bass." *And maybe*, I think to myself, *we like sounding like shit, you note-reader, mouth-breather, English-eggs-and-beans-eating fucker.*

THERE WITH YOU

I don't have much to do once we finish in the studio, and we still have two weeks before a big concert, scheduled right before Christmas. So I walk around all day long. Occasionally, Lori comes with. Yeah, I am in London, which sounds good, but it's all drizzle and eggs and beans when you have no cash and way too much time.

I call Joe on a rainy afternoon. The sounds of drops like percussion on the phone booth, U.K. sirens, people passing on the street. A British lady's voice asks for my phone card number. The phone rings.

After Halloween, Joe offered to move to Minneapolis, but I know he didn't really want to. He's lived in California his whole life, and Minneapolis is actually pretty weak if you aren't used to it—the long winters, the insular vibe. I'm not even there most of the time. But we don't know how to move on either.

Joe moved out of his apartment and into Henry's house. This seems like a positive shift. Change as the catalyst for forward motion, this is something we both believe in. He is dating some girl from France or somewhere like that. She is a model or a photographer or a waitress or an actress. He tells me he only wants to be with me. This is exactly what I want to hear. But I don't know how to gain access to my rational brain. There is only emotion, this sense of isolation that I fear will become permanent. There is only praying he'll pick up the phone.

"Hi, Little Leon."

"How's your stupid-ass French girlfriend?"

"You're my girlfriend. How are all your stupid boy-friends?"

"Still stupid."

"That's what I thought."

"In *NME* there's a story about us. They call us 'old hags.' No one here likes us anymore. They like Hole now."

"Don't worry about that. That's just how it is in England."

"I don't know how to not worry. I'd rather cry in an English pay phone booth instead."

"Don't cry, Leon."

"I hate it here. This place makes me sad."

"I wish I was there with you."

BRIGHTON

Kat, Lori, and I split some money from the label. I decide to take the train to Brighton, about fifty miles south of London, on the coast. I am told how pretty and tranquil it is there. I call Joe before I leave and his number is disconnected. I figure he didn't pay the bill and take this as a sign that it's time to create a little distance between us.

I find a bed and breakfast: old English lady, cups of tea, a simple dining room. I go to the store and get wine, snacks, and magazines and make my place extra cozy. I take a long walk along the beach and eat dinner at a small restaurant by the sea. I return.

The phone in the hall releases a loud English ring.

It's for me.

It's John Loder.

"Something terrible has happened."

I try to call my mom but have trouble dialing the long series of numbers on my calling card, taking several tries before getting it right. I am crying and hollering into the phone. She can't understand what I am saying. Everything is happening both slow and fast, leaden and light. I sit on the steps near the B&B kitchen, making a scene in this polite and quiet place.

"Please tell me what to do."

She says, come home.

I put my things in my bag. I tell the innkeeper I have to go. I'm not sure why I tell her someone in my family died.

She calls a taxi to take me to the train station. She won't look at me.

At the depot, I ask the man at the ticket desk which train I should take back to London. I walk toward the platform and forget which one he said. I go back to the desk. I do this two or three times. He finally walks me to the right spot.

I sit all the way in the back and hold my knees tight to my chest, my head leaning on the window. People approach to sit next to me, take a close glance at my expression, and sit somewhere else. No one asks if I'm OK.

Lori and John are waiting for me at the station in London. I go to them, sobbing, snot, no words.

Crumpling to the ground, standing back up. It is busy in the station, but the three of us are still, standing there for a while. I am buried between their chests, motion all around us, people annoyed we are in the way.

"Let's go home," someone finally says.

MARROW FROM MY BONES

PUNK ROCK BAND'S ROAD CREW MEMBER SLAIN
Los Angeles Times, Metro Digest / Local News in Brief
December 20, 1991

A Venice man who once served on the road crew for the defunct punk rock band Black Flag was shot to death Thursday by robbers as he walked home from a neighborhood grocery store, police said.

Joe Cole, 30, and his roommate were returning from the Boys Market on Lincoln Boulevard at 12:40 a.m. when they were robbed of about $40 by two gunmen, said Lt. Ross Moen. The victims were then ordered to return to their house about 1½ blocks away, where one of the suspects fired a single shot at Cole and fled, Moen said.

Cole, the son of TV actor Dennis Cole, was a "roadie" for Black Flag during the critically acclaimed group's final U.S. tour in 1986. David Crouch, manager of Rhino Records in Westwood, described Cole as a popular figure in the alternative music scene who had been a "confidant and right-hand man" to the musicians in Black Flag.

HOPKINS, PUBLIC AND PRIVATE

It storms hard and the snow is so high that you can hardly open your front door, that year just after you turned eight. Listening to WCCO radio in the morning to hear the school closing announcements, yelling "HOORAY!" when they call out, "Hopkins, public and private." Your mom puts on her cross-country skis and goes to the store, where groceries are now called "supplies." You dress real warm and head out to find all the other kids on the block. Taking sleds out of garages and sliding down hills. Getting out the K-tel block-maker you ordered off of TV and building a snow fort in the front yard, a little entrance, a snug place to hide.

Your mom makes french onion soup, the way she learned when she lived in Orléans, France—one of the only dishes she makes. She gets the brown crocks down from above the stove, the ones that have their own little tops. She prepares the broth, first sautéing onions, then adding white wine and beef stock, letting it simmer. Ladling the soup into the crocks filled with garlic round crackers, putting Gruyère cheese over the top, and placing the bowls in the oven.

Even with your fingers frozen and your cheeks glowing red, you stay in your snow fort until your mom yells out the front door, "Time to come in!" And then you run because you know her soup is ready.

NOWHERE I WANT TO BE

I fly back from England immediately. Everyone seems surprised when I choose to cancel the Christmas show, but I might miss his funeral if I stay. Lori offers to come along, to fly home too. She wants to be there for me, but I need to go by myself. Kat hasn't called. She was out when I left for the airport, and I haven't heard anything from her. I don't hear anything from her for weeks, not until our first practice back in Minneapolis.

Henry comes to the airport to pick me up, and my friend Janet from New York shows up too. I feel like an asshole because I didn't get a hold of Henry to tell him I already had a ride, and now I have wasted his time. He's annoyed, even though he is trying not to be. I feel needy and weird and there is nowhere I want to be. This is something I would have called Joe about, and he would have made me feel better.

Henry takes me to his house, where the shooting took place. We walk down the sidewalk, stained with Joe's blood, to go inside. He tells me that one day when I am somewhere, like in a grocery store parking lot, I may double over and cry. "It's just going to hit you," he says.

Henry gives me a box of Joe's stuff, pictures of us mostly, including some Polaroids Joe had of me partially undressed, adding mortification to the list of emotions I am experiencing. Henry was more like Joe's girlfriend than I was. I'm the one who hurt him. I shouldn't even be here.

A SILVER LATCH

His death feels like rejection.

The feeling is alive with the pictures, magazines, and concert flyers I keep in a blue '60s suitcase, a silver latch that will not close.

He used to run through the deep sand. A way of running that uses more energy while building strength. It must feel claustrophobic being sucked into the earth that way, like bolting up the stairs of my parents' basement, imagining demons chasing me, not able to get to the door that opened into our bright yellow kitchen fast enough.

Joe is not defined by any particular moment. He is those pictures I keep: a teenager holding a puppy, in his twenties on the road with his best friends, thirty and sitting by my side in front of my parents' fireplace.

Before he died, the status of our relationship was completely unclear, that tricky place that is usually resolved with time. His death is not a resolution. I have dreams where he calls me, the phone disconnects as we try to talk; I wake up. I dream that he faked his death and returns.

They went out to rent a video and get groceries to make sandwiches, I was told. Joe put his bread in the toaster before they left.

THE NATURE OF THE WOUND

Nothing can kill your Spirit Joe
Sleep with love my friend.
—FROM *A SONG FOR JOE* BY HUBERT SELBY JR.

I wonder if he realized what was about to happen. When a bullet goes into someone's head, how does that work? Does the heart stop first, while the blood continues to circulate?

I view his body alone.

He looks like a wax figure, his face reconstructed due to the nature of the wound, mouth twisted upward in a smirk. I approach the casket and kiss his forehead, his body indifferent, made out of clay.

I feel inanimate, too, in that room with pacifying music piped in, the couches and Kleenex boxes meant to evoke home. The gentle voices of the funeral directors. The poem Hubert Selby Jr. wrote for the service.

Joe's bottomless silence.

At the graveside service, I realize that I barely know any of his friends. Beverly Hills cemetery, green grass and hills, the afternoon light, the urn on a stand, ash and bone. Strangers weeping. I leave flowers at the gravesite.

Joe's mom, Sally, knows about all of our problems, so I am touched when she invites me to ride in the limo back to a relative's house where the family is gathering. A cousin confides that Joe told him years before that he knew he'd die when he was thirty.

Later that night, Sally and Joe's younger sister, Staci, and I go to see Henry perform at a club. He tells the story of the murder in great detail. I want to protect them from hearing this, but all we can do is stand there, holding hands, staring. After the show, Sally tells Henry that he has to be her son now. Henry doesn't know what to say.

Joe's case is later on *Unsolved Mysteries*. I see the news footage from that night: his body on a gurney covered with a sheet being lifted into the back of an ambulance.

I wonder if the Spanish-style bungalow he lived in will be hard to sell after the murder. I wonder if young families will be afraid of his ghost.

I wonder if I am.

23

I talk about Joe. I talk about him a lot. I make people uncomfortable.

Bill Phelps, a friend from Minneapolis who is now a famous photographer, takes the cover shot for our *Peel Sessions* record shortly after Joe's death. My hair is in my face, the way it always is in photos taken around that time. Men tell me it's sexy, but all I see is myself trying to disappear.

"You know, sometimes when your life goes that direction, it stays that way forever," Kat says to me at our next practice, a few weeks after Joe's death. To her, this is not necessarily a negative thing, or so it seemed.

Lori, Kat, and I steep, become infected. Lately, we barely talk at all. Sadness turned to awkwardness, then frustration, anger, toxicity. I am especially bitter and relentless in airing my discontent. Whoever isn't in the room gets bad-mouthed by the other two.

"Kat thinks she's the queen."

"Lori is so fucking cheap."

"Michelle needs to get over it."

Lori is so mad at me. Kat is completely emotionally vacant, gone. I don't know how to handle being rejected by these two. I thought we were supposed to take care of each other like sisters. I've been wishing that I was the one who died.

We have a three-week tour scheduled to begin in a few weeks opening for Dinosaur Jr. and My Bloody Valentine.

Big clubs, good money, and we love these two bands. But I haven't slept or eaten well in weeks: skinny, pale, stringy hair. I buy pants from the children's section of the thrift store. But I don't feel like I can say no to going on this tour. The way you get respect after someone close to you dies is to persevere, be strong, just keep going. I want to be like that.

I say I'll go if we three girls can have one room, with Howard and our soundman, Scott, in another. I need to sleep; the insomnia has lasted for weeks. When I do drift off, I have nightmares, and I don't want to sleep in a room with a shit-ton of other people.

The first night of the tour, Lori returns from the motel check-in with one key, not acknowledging our room agreement. Howard and I take one bed, the other for Lori and Kat, who are out with the other bands. Scott is on the floor.

In the middle of the night, the girls return, lights switched on, wasted, loudly riffling through their bags, waking us all up.

"Shut the fuck up!" says Scott.

"You shut the fuck up!" they say.

Howard and I stay quiet. Lori and Kat set off again, leaving the lights on. Howard and I look at each other.

"What was that about?" I ask him.

"Shut the fuck up!" Scott yells at us.

We shut the fuck up. Lying in bed next to Howard; he holds my sweaty hand. I stare hard at the ceiling. Midnight marks my twenty-third birthday. J Mascis from Dinosaur Jr. brings a cake to soundcheck that night.

I BELIEVE

I am dissolving.

People are talking to me but I don't understand their words. Ordering a cup of coffee has become a challenge, afraid I will forget how to talk, sure I am going to choke on my sip. The neck of my bass is warped from playing so hard, and I am constantly out of tune. Lori and Kat think I'm fucking up on purpose and glare at me during our sets.

I call Joe's number from a pay phone and listen to the this-number-has-been-disconnected message.

Several months before he died, Joe cut his long hair and sent me his thick locks in the mail. I travel with some of his mane in an envelope, hidden way at the bottom of my suitcase. I don't tell anyone about my stash.

We arrive at the next club. I ask the promoter if there is a pool nearby and he takes me to the local university. The sharp smell of chlorine and the echo of the enormous empty room create balance as I slip under the water, and then begin to swim:

I believe water can heal.

I believe Joe is watching me.

I believe if I listen carefully I will hear him, sending sonar signals through the waves, calling my name.

Kinetic energy, motion, and repetition eventually cut through the buzz.

MY SISTER

Things are bad between us as we pull the van into the parking lot of the Austin Motel, which has a neon sign that looks like a giant penis. We picked this place because it's only $25 a night. A few of the rooms have the curtains open and the lights on. In one of the windows an oily naked man holds his erect penis; he's just standing there, muscly, cheesy with tan skin and long dark hair, smiling at us as his enormous and grotesque boner shines in the glow of lamplight.

"Fuck!" and "Gross!" and "No!" we all yell at once. Hands over eyes, then hands off of eyes for another look and more yelling. We are too tired to find another place to stay, and $25 rooms are hard to find. We get two rooms tonight because we played a show opening for L7 and they generously gave us a big bonus. Kat and I share one room; Lori gets her own.

We open our doors and duck in, locking up behind us, hooking the latches, closing the pleated drapes by pulling the cords. Our room has pink carpeting worn down to gum, and it smells like flooded basement, old man, and ashtray. We stopped at a gas station and bought beer on our way back from the club. The best decision of the day.

Kat and I actually dig the zebra print bedspread of our queen-sized bed, though it loses its appeal when pulled back to reveal dirty-dishwater-colored sheets topped with several dark pubes. More yelling. We pull the spread back up and decide to sleep on top.

Cars keep coming and going; doors opening and closing. A man and woman are fighting outside our door. We can't stop thinking about boner man being so near, but soon we are tipsy and cracking up as we hear people fucking. Men grunting, ladies moaning, doors opening and closing.

We each open another beer.

I start jumping on the bed in my underwear and t-shirt. Kat takes a Polaroid as I fly, air bound, gymnast-style, arms stretched above my head, knees bent, feet to the side, sailing high above the geometrics of pretend zebra skin. She gives the photo that special little shake, and soon this picture travels in her suitcase through at least twelve states, all the way to her velvety lady apartment, and into the hands of her druggie boyfriend, who tacks it onto the wall of his band's practice space, right above his amp covered in beer cans and set lists, where it hangs for months, the most stupid smile on my face as I float in the air like a hummingbird.

We drink enough that we tell each other things we like boys to do during sex, something I am usually too shy to talk about. Soon one of us will puke in the dismal bathroom, but for now we are just relieved to be getting along.

"You're my sister," I say.

Kat performing on stage, 1991

NOTHING IS THE SAME

We're loading into the club in San Francisco when he shows up, his head down as he approaches, long chestnut hair falling into his face. A boy version of Kat. I know she wrote "Dust Cake Boy" about this one, the chorus repeating the words, "He fucks mean." But otherwise she's secretive about their relationship, which seems druggie, but with something darker too. This tour is already a total ruin. I feel like it's about to get worse.

In the morning, we wake up at a friend's house; all of us except Kat, who disappeared after our set. We have no idea how to find her, and we're all ready to go. Lori says we should just go back to Minneapolis even though we have a few shows left on the tour—fuck it, let's go home. She says we should leave Kat in California.

"No fucking way are we leaving her here," Howard says.

I want to find Kat *and* go home, but more importantly I need to get out of there. I can't handle the stress, and the way everyone's acting psycho and pissed off. And they are so sick of my bitching and bummer face. It's going to take the band a couple of days to drive to our next concert in Chicago, so I decide to stay and visit Joe's mom, Sally, in Tiburon and then fly there. I don't care how much it costs. They don't seem to give a shit if I stay or go, so I catch a cab and leave them behind.

Lori makes a bunch of phone calls. Howard has no idea how, but she finds someone who knows where Kat is. They get the address and head over.

Howard calls me later, disturbed by what he saw. He says they found Kat passed out in a creepy apartment with the guy, a radio blaring static, the scene feeling evil and acid-drenched. Howard carried her out to the van.

I'm grateful not to have witnessed this. Still, I feel responsible because I wasn't there, because I make everyone sad, because I saturate them with loss. I never ask Kat what happened or if she is all right. And nothing is the same after that.

INCOMPLETE

Sometimes when a tree is diseased, fungus infiltrates green leaves, turning them yellow, and they fall to the ground. Root systems become unstable, growth stunted.

Thriving in a profession where people applaud and yell your name each night might provide a clue to what needs were being met, while also indicating the place where my development started to wither.

Knowing how rare it is to become a perennial in the music business always left me wondering what the end was going to look like, when it might come. How was I going to take care of myself without any other skills, never really knowing anything else in my adult life but being a musician?

There are a lot of reasons why I quit the band. Usually attributed to grief when I read strangers' explanations of it, as I often do.

This is mostly true.

It was Lori's fault for just wanting me to get over it.

This is mostly true.

It was Kat's fault for not standing up for me.

This is mostly true.

It was my fault for not being stronger, grieving better.

This is mostly true.

We start recording the album that becomes *Fontanelle* with Lee from Sonic Youth producing. For the first time, I am confident about my bass playing. I don't just hit the same notes as Kat, I create skillful melodies. When Kat and I work on the songs together, the chemistry is absolute and pure. We are somehow able to ignore everything else that is happening when we collaborate.

In the past, Lori and I always accepted and encouraged each other musically—it was easy and natural to connect—but now, we're both so resentful. It's impossible to put the caustic feelings aside. Still, I feel so comfortable on bass. I am not worried what anyone thinks, knowing I've actually become a good musician. It's confusing to feel so competent and creative, while so emotionally shut down. The remoteness makes me feel uninhibited in a way, allowing me to work through the pain, while also making my decision more agonizing.

I don't think they care if I stay or if I go.

I want to prove that I can give up all the attention and remain spiritually and emotionally intact. I want to prove that I don't need the superficial acceptance. A garden and a dog is all I need.

I can't do this anymore.

Kat and I talk at her home, both of us crying. I leave Lori a letter in her mailbox.

What I don't realize is how these roots are gnarled and deep, pulling them out more painful than I can imagine. The way all those years will feel forever incomplete.

FILL THE PLACE

After I leave the band, I continue wandering, packing up my beloved purple Dodge Dart with clothes tossed into a laundry basket, a futon, a lamp, a small black-and-white TV. I have no idea what I am doing, but trust the answer will eventually arrive.

I drive out to California and stay with Sally in Tiburon. The two of us smoke Virginia Slims and drink wine in front of the TV at night. We wear curlers and paint our nails. I sleep in the guest bedroom under a quilt sewn by Joe's grandmother. I give Sally some of Joe's hair, which she keeps in a jewelry box in the bathroom.

My mom calls but does not acknowledge Sally, simply asking for me when Sally answers the phone, threatened by our closeness, unnerved by Sally's grief. I tell my mom that everything is going to be fine.

When I get a job as an usher at a theater that presents the same corny musical each night, Sally irons the white button-down shirts I wear. I take a second job bartending at a restaurant in North Beach while still working at the theater on weekend afternoons, plus a third job mornings at a coffeehouse, where I heat scones and mop the floor at 5 a.m. At the bar, I look up recipes in my drink guide when the tourists order their cocktails because I lied on my application, saying I had bartended before. I am the slowest drink mixer in the world and this does not go unnoticed. I start pouring Kahlúa in my coffee when no one is looking.

Washing my Dodge Dart, bought from Howard for $500

I save enough money to rent a studio apartment in San Francisco, thrilled when I find a '50s-era kitchen table and wobbly wooden chair at a yard sale, then an old turquoise loveseat on the curb, enough furniture to fill the place. Taking the bus in both the dark of night and the early morning after selling the Dart because there is nowhere to park. Coming back to my home, falling asleep with the TV on, emerging the next day. Working as much as possible, I try to be a good employee, always wanting to stay busy. I scrub everything shiny clean.

I go to see the band Superchunk play and watch their bassist, Laura, jump up and down so joyfully. Loss flows through me like a stream. I drink a beer, then two, then three, before bed each night.

TIDBIT SOUP

I send Lori a letter after writing about twenty drafts, trying to make it as open and kind as possible while being honest about my still-lingering anger. She writes back weeks later, saying only that I was making her the scapegoat, not acknowledging anything I had said or all that had gone down.

On Sunday afternoons, I wander around the Mission District, getting a burrito at La Cumbre, then heading back to my neighborhood near the Castro. Hanging out at the big record store on Market Street. I know I shouldn't, but I can't help but page through the magazines looking for stories about Babes in Toyland. I once see a few lines in *Spin*, in the gossip column called "Tidbit Soup," explaining that I left the band because of my inability to cope with my boyfriend's murder. I see an article in *NME*, a picture of me sipping a drink through a straw with a sad look on my face, the headline reading "Bass Player Sacked," the article saying I got fired because I was such a pain in the ass. I see a picture of the band without me, another girl standing in my place.

Tim Carr calls and tells me he'll help me if I want to start my own band, he believes in me that much.

A letter arrives, thoughtful and gracious, telling me how no one will forget me or all the hard work I had done for the band. It was written by their new bassist, Maureen.

CINDY FUCKING SHERMAN

The full-length album *Fontanelle* is released, and the band plays a big show in Loring Park in Minneapolis to celebrate. Lori's dad died the night before, yet she doesn't cancel the show. Lori always had a difficult relationship with her father, but he planned on coming to the concert and bringing all his buddies before he had a heart attack. About eighty of his friends still show up to support her and honor him. I wish I could have been there for her too.

Babes in Toyland now have a manager, who sends me a cassette of *Fontanelle* in the mail. When I open the package, I look at the thank-yous in the liner notes and I am first; the feeling is wistful relief. Then I look at the cover artwork, a photo of a baby doll. Enough with the baby dolls. I read the lyrics and look at the credits. I see that Cindy Sherman took the photo and I think of that day in London when Joe and I were fighting and I went to the Cindy Sherman exhibit alone. Lori and Kat didn't want to go—they didn't know who Cindy Sherman was. But they knew she was my favorite; the feeling is betrayal.

I go to work.

The story that Cindy Sherman photos tell me is about the way women are viewed, their vulnerabilities, the roles they play, how scary it is for them to age. I think of Kat screaming like in a slasher picture. I think of Lori beating the shit out of her drums. I think of how many things we are, how complicated, the way we act around men, the way we treat each other. Fuck doll babies. Why would you pick that when you had Cindy Sherman? Fuck everything. I think about Cindy Sherman as I mop the fucking floor. I think about Cindy Sherman as I pour Kahlúa in my coffee. I think about Cindy Sherman as I take out the trash. I think about Cindy Sherman as I scrub everything shiny clean. I think about her on the bus ride home.

I later hear it was Tim Carr's idea. I bet they talked about it while eating lobsters at Manny's.

WE ARE ONE

My family is really worried about me being on my own, so I just keep telling them how well everything is going. I have a few friends here in San Francisco, people I met on tour, but now that I'm not in the band they treat me differently, like I'm not that interesting anymore.

I need to be with people, yet the moment they are around, I want to be alone. A distressed aura emanates from my body like the rays of the sun—muted colors and a low hum. And that's a drag for folks to be around on a summer day.

One night I go with some friends to see *1991: The Year Punk Broke,* Dave Markey's documentary about Sonic Youth that includes footage of Babes in Toyland performing at Reading. When I see the opening credits, it's like a dream, my name written across the big screen.

We play "Dust Cake Boy," the three of us in front of that enormous crowd, the shot switching swiftly between Kat and me. She screams into the mic and I spin around, edited together like blinking your eyes, she and I, as if we are one.

When Dinosaur Jr. plays, there's a shot of Joe and me, his arms wrapped around me, our heads bobbing together to the music while we watch from the side of the stage. We're beaming. This fleeting moment appears from the ether as I sit in the dark theater trying to breathe. One of my friends nudges me, leaning over and whispering, "Hey, look, it's you."

Joe and me at the Reading Festival, on the day **The Year Punk Broke** *was filmed, 1991; this photo was taken by the filmmaker, Dave Markey.*

THIEF PEOPLE

I get fired from my bartending job because I don't know how to make cocktails and I am caught giving a regular customer a free tap beer. The owner says, "I don't hire thief people." I am a thief people. I am a bad person who is also too stupid to make drinks.

I go to the pub next door, ordering a beer, smoking a menthol cigarette, and staring. I really needed that job. A note comes my way from the beautiful California boy sitting at the end of the bar. It says, "You are pretty. Can I have a smoke?" He is a ballet dancer and a surfer with soft curls and blue eyes. He is a perfect boy. He moves over to the stool next to mine. We drink a few more beers, leave the bar, and walk across town. The hills of San Francisco, the views of the bay, the Victorian houses all nestled together, the streetcars passing by. He tells me about his life, his family, the harsh breakup he just went through. I tell him about the band, why I am here in California. I tell him all about Joe. He doesn't think I'm dumb or a thief people. He thinks I am incredible. He walks me home.

The next day he calls and asks if I want to go to a party with him that weekend, he wants to introduce me to all his friends. I say I'll go.

But I don't go. Not answering the buzzer, not picking up the phone, throwing away the notes he leaves at my door.

CONSTANT MOTION

I realize there are no answers to be discovered in San Francisco, so it's time to leave. I return the loveseat to the curb, along with the table and chair for a new owner to find. Stopping in Tiburon to say good-bye to Sally is the hardest part.

I rent a car with plans to go back to Minneapolis. But when I get a few hours away, I can't do it. I can't go back, believing my survival depends on constant motion.

With just a few bucks saved, I head to New Orleans, for me a utopia of creativity and freedom, a place animated with color and smoke, haunted and sexy. I remember the way my spirit rose when we drove across the long bridges over the waterways and swamps each time the band arrived to play a show. That same energy is infused with promise as I arrive on my own. This quickly morphs into fear when I realize, again, I have no idea what I'm doing.

The fearful undercurrent in my mother's voice travels through the Bell South pay phone receiver when I call to tell her I'm not coming home.

"What are you going to do for money?"

"I have a friend who runs a bar here. I can work there," I lie.

I tuck my bag under the bed at a youth hostel and keep the car a few more days. I check out a room for rent in a boardinghouse. One tenant has his door open, revealing empty bottles and dirty blankets, the thick animal smell

179

of stew cooking on a hot plate, claustrophobic cigarette smoke, poverty.

I spend a few days looking for jobs, but no one is hiring. I see the HELP WANTED sign on the door of Big Daddy's in the French Quarter, the strip club with mechanical fishnet-clad legs swinging in and out of a fake window at the entrance. I tell the manager I've stripped before. He says I can start at 6 p.m.

Here is where the story could turn sordid and sad: cocaine and blowjobs, mascara running down my face. But suppose the girl in this story doesn't show up for that shift at the strip club. She doesn't rent the pitiful room. What if instead she walks around the French Quarter all night with new friends she made at the youth hostel, and they come home and laugh in their bunk beds? What if she finds a dirt-cheap, one-room apartment in a beautiful brick building in the French Quarter, with a little balcony where she can keep a few plants? And what if she gets a job at the flower shop around the corner? Suppose her parents send a few bucks to get the electricity and phone turned on. If all those things happen, could her loneliness still be considered tragic? What if she sometimes drinks until she dissolves and goes home with boys from the bar, ones who aren't that great, and she can't find her bra in the morning? Imagine her taking mushrooms that the guy in the next apartment gives her, tripping and sitting on that balcony as fireworks burst over the Mississippi. What if she watches those fireworks alone on New Year's Eve as she thinks of him, whispers her thoughts to him, the boy dead for over two years now? What if she does this while wearing her fanciest dress?

Balcony of my New Orleans apartment, 1993

HEAVENLY AND DEEP

I work my ass off at Tommy's Flowers on Chartres Street in the French Quarter, always needing a task. In the morning, opening the big green shutters of the storefront; putting the buckets of mixed bouquets on the sidewalk; unwrapping the orchids, freesia, anemone, hydrangea, and tulips from their crinkly plastic sleeves, fresh from California, Hawaii, and South America; giving each flower a fresh cut, and placing them in a bucket for a drink. Crushing the thick stems of the blooming branches with a hammer so they'll sip water; stripping the roses clean of thorns; wiring the bright gerbera daisies so they stand up straight; pulling the orange and purple plumes of the birds-of-paradise out of their green beaks. I put all the blooms out on the sales floor, arranged by color.

I remove the day-old flowers, emptying the buckets into the street like an old washerwoman and scrubbing them with bleach. I sweep up leaves, stems, and petals and throw them in the trash, using my foot to squish everything down. After breaking down the boxes, I haul them out to the curb for the garbage truck that drives through the Quarter each day, the garbage men hollering and singing, clanging musically on garbage can lids and the side of the truck; you can hear them coming from blocks away. Answering the phone, a flower tucked behind my ear: "Tommy's Flowers, this is Michelle."

The New Orleans air is humid and rich, and the shop smells earthy, not the sad smell of hospital carnations, but heavenly and deep. I never let Tommy throw any flowers away; bedraggled blooms in twenty-five-cent vases from the church thrift store fill my place.

For my birthday, Tommy gives me a bouquet of stargazer lilies, the most expensive blooms in the shop. He teaches me how to arrange flowers, from the little bud vases we make each week for the restaurant tables to the big flowing bouquets we create for extravagant weddings held in French Quarter hotel ballrooms or thickly pillared antebellum mansions. I create corsages and boutonnieres, head wreaths, altarpieces, aisle markers, funeral sprays, baskets, and centerpieces—long-and-lows for rectangular tables, and roundy-moundys for circular. We are always busy.

The fancy people from the Quarter love my flower arrangements. "They like you for some reason," Tommy jokes, "I don't really get it."

He calls me the Thrift Store Dead Flower Queen.

I wear my vintage dresses or bell-bottom Levi's cords from the '70s and vintage lace blouses, Converse All Stars, and hardly ever brush my hair. These are rich southern ladies with flawless coifs and big jewelry, drinking in the daytime. I have no idea why they like me either.

Tommy's dog, Champ, a hound mix, hangs out in the shop most of the time, but occasionally he meanders outside, taking himself for walks down to the Mississippi River and later returning, yawning, and stretching his legs before falling asleep in his favorite spot in the workroom in the back. I sometimes lie on the floor next to Champ and kiss his furry head, which he just barely tolerates.

With the staff at Tommy's Flowers, New Orleans, 1993

Tommy has a sweet '50s red pickup truck. I sit in the back with our teenage delivery boy and hold on to the big arrangements, making sure they don't tip as we head out to set up events. Tommy lives above the flower shop. He goes up to his apartment quite often, needing to lie down and take a nap. He gets sick a lot but won't tell me what's wrong.

Some days, after the shop closes, we smoke weed in his pad and come back down to the workroom, staying late making centerpieces for Mardi Gras parties; purple, green, and yellow flowers, masks and feathers on sticks, glitter everywhere. The other employees have parties to go to and friends to meet, but I stay until all the orders are done while drunk midwestern boys pee on our shop. Neither Tommy nor I care at all about Mardi Gras. We can't wait until it is over. He is a really good friend, from the Midwest too, telling me about his boyfriends and his childhood. I tell him everything.

I USED TO BE IN A BAND

On my days off, I walk around the neighborhood. I never tire of staring at the ornate scrolling ironwork, the rust-colored brick of the old buildings, or the flickering gas lanterns lighting up the doorways. I peek between the buildings trying to get a glimpse of the elaborate court-yards hidden deep inside, some with old copper sugar kettles used as fountains and gardens filled with banana trees, wild azaleas, and ginger.

I walk by the French Market and Café du Monde and watch the tourists. I have coffee at Kaldi's and buy a prayer candle at Marie Laveau's House of Voodoo. I stop at Pres-ervation Hall and listen from the sidewalk to the band inside.

When I can't sleep, which is quite often, I go to the gay bar across the street from my apartment, which is open twenty-four hours. I've become friends with the bar-tender. He tells the occasional frat boys who mistakenly wander into the place to leave me alone.

I meet a boy at the laundromat/bar where I wash my clothes on Sunday afternoons. Young with long dark hair, baby faced and pretty, small and non-threatening. I tell him I used to be in a band.

We drink beer and play pool for hours, singing along to the jukebox. Later stumbling arm in arm out of the bar and driving in a beat-to-shit car back to his place outside my bubble of the French Quarter.

The blight of New Orleans surrounds us as we pass houses with broken windows, peeling paint, and rotting wood. Vines with thick claws devour small shacks, roofs are caved in, doors wide open reveal bare mattresses on the floor. Men are drinking 40-ouncers and grilling in their front yards, joking and slapping each other on the back. They holler, "Hey girl," as teenagers walk by in tight jeans and high heels.

Inside his shotgun shack, those weedy vines are creeping in the cracks of the bargeboard siding. There are water stains on the ceiling, and the place smells of mold. The July heat is suffocating, motionless. Beams of early evening light strain to enter beneath the yellowing window shade as an orange tabby nuzzles me, the fur sticking to my sweaty legs. The boy and I drink some more.

At first I am apathetic toward the inevitable sex. I want to listen to records, but he is persistent and a really soft kisser, and everything starts to smolder as I fill with lightness and ache. I sit on the edge of his bed as he kneels on the floor. I guide his head under my sundress.

The moment reduces to ash as soon as I come. Now there is no exiting this house fast enough.

"Can I get a ride home?"

He is angry at my lack of reciprocation, so I let him fuck me. As soon as he is finished, I look for my purse to leave. But I am having a hard time inhaling and start to panic. I go outside and sit on the front stoop. The wheezing is sharp. I cannot get a sip of air. Red-hot blood flows to my face and I start crying, which makes the gasping much worse. The kids playing in the street are laughing at me.

The guy takes me to the hospital. Asthma attack, they say. I don't have asthma or insurance, I tell the nurse as she fixes me with oxygen and sedation, warm lungs again full of breath, the welcome druggie haze. Gentle prayers of Jesus travel through me softly as they float out of the loud-speaker. The boy stays at the hospital until I am released a few hours later. He takes me home. I don't want him to know where I live, but I am so tired as he tucks me into my bed and closes the door lightly behind him as he leaves.

Tommy is the only person I tell about the hospital. He takes me to his favorite bar that night after work, the place that allows dogs. Champ lies at our feet. I tell him I have to go home. He tells me he doesn't want me to leave.

I have been waiting so long for someone to say those words to me.

DEAD FLOWERS

I stop by the shop to say good-bye to Tommy before leaving town.

This is the part where I want to tell you how hard it is to leave New Orleans. Cleaning my place until it sparkles, using a scrub brush and bleach, even taking the streetcar uptown to get the right shade of white to touch up the paint because I really need my damage deposit back.

I want to describe the three days it takes to get home to Minneapolis, driving an economy rental car. Winding my way back out of the South through the waterways where the cypresses grow, knotty and prehistoric, rising from the swamps like the living dead.

I want you to feel as I feel passing the rickety old houses, vintage diners, and abandoned drive-in movie theaters in lost little back-road towns. Traveling on the highway past Jackson, Mississippi, and Memphis, Tennessee, as I creep up that route along the Mississippi River.

I want you to picture the cheap motel room where I take a hot bath and get into bed, building a nook with the pillows, pulling the stiff sheets up close to my chin. And the lecherous truck driver in Missouri who scares the shit out of me as I tweak on my third cup of shitty coffee, riding my bumper and honking his angry horn, pulling up next to me with an exaggerated smile and lunkhead wave. The way I give him the finger and spill my coffee on the beige carpet, leaving a sad stain on the floor.

I want you to imagine the volume cranked up on the classic rock stations that tune in as I pass through cities and then turn to static, and how I sing along. And taking a break at a truck stop in Cedar Rapids, Iowa—so close to home—and calling my parents from the row of pay phones, letting them know when to expect me while I draw daisies on the phone book.

I want you to understand how I both do and do not want to arrive.

But I don't really remember any of those things precisely, although they are all real enough to belong in this time-altered truth. Here is what I do recall: Tommy filling my rental car with dead flowers before I left. I remember the way those wilted blooms lay on the dash and back window during the long ride home.

THE HOUSE BEHIND YOURS

You're eleven years old, in your backyard on Hobby Oak Drive. The springtime sun is shining, everything turning green after the long winter. Below your feet is grass, dandelions, bright and pretty, roots reaching to the center of the world. You wonder why people hate those flowers. Beyond the sky is the spirit you talk to, saying you're sorry when you're bad, asking for things you want or help when you need it.

There's the garden you planted with your dad. You check each day to see how much everything has grown.

Your mother tells you how special you are, how you are smart enough to be anything you want to be, but you don't believe her. You really couldn't be a doctor or a lawyer. The way you feel invisible, like you are and will always be nothing. You don't know how to explain these feelings to anyone.

The air is flowery from the cherry tree that blossoms earliest each spring. You pluck pink blooms, throw them in the air, and watch them float to the ground. They smell sweet and strong like lady perfume. You walk through the bushes into the yard of the house behind yours. You play with a seesaw, hidden by the overgrown brush, pushing one side down, then the other. The people in that house had a daughter, but she died when she was your age, a very long time ago. When you see lights on in their windows at night, you get scared, thinking the dead girl is signaling you from her bedroom, trying to tell you that she needs someone to talk to.

WIENER WATER TEA HOUSE

I get back from New Orleans and stay in my parents' basement. Humiliation. Waking up in the guest bedroom surrounded by school yearbook pictures, dehumidifiers, and a rowing machine. At night, I borrow my mom's car to go see my friends in the city. It really does feel good to be around my old friends.

Babes in Toyland go on the Lollapalooza tour with Alice in Chains, Primus, and Dinosaur Jr. When the tour comes to St. Paul, I hang out with Kat after the show, intentionally showing up late so I don't have to watch them perform.

Lori later calls from the road to tell me Kat OD'd. "She turned blue and died. Then they revived her," she said. Kat acting like it's no big deal while everyone around her was totally shattered.

Kat marries Stu, the singer from the Australian noise band Lubricated Goat, and moves to Seattle. Maureen lives in Chicago, while Lori remains in Minneapolis. Lori and I are polite when we run into each other.

I rent an apartment and get a job at a flower shop a few blocks away in Calhoun Square, the mall in Uptown that everyone hates because they tore down all the little shops to build it. I work between a yuppie restaurant that serves carpaccio and mussels and a place that sells only socks. I make the customers mixed bouquets or wrap up single roses. Sometimes no one comes in for hours, so I make wreaths with hot glue and dried flowers. When the walls are filled, I clean, dusting the tops and scrubbing the insides of the coolers. Friends stop by often, and sometimes strangers ask, "Didn't you used to be in Babes in Toyland?"

The mall is right across the street from the Uptown Bar, so I head over and see bands after I lock the glass doors of the flower shop at 9 p.m. Always feeling conspicuously alone, I am overfriendly to everyone to prove just how great I am doing.

I buy a cheap, beat-up red Ranchero from a guy who was nice enough to let me make a few payments. I paint the walls in my apartment burgundy and hang thrift store paintings of flowers, bowls of fruit, and the Virgin Mary, even though I'm Jewish. Smiling fish, seahorse, and mermaid plaques from the '50s on the bathroom walls.

Before Kat left for Seattle, she gave up her place in Minneapolis because she was traveling so much. When she comes back to town, she stays with me, sleeping on my couch. We call ourselves crazy old lady sisters, and this is the best we have ever gotten along. We have boyfriends who are best friends and we all hang out together in the one-room apartment listening to music.

Neither of us cooks much, so we eat tea and toast, fried eggs, and many hot dogs. One morning our tea tastes both floral and savory; I realize I made it using old hot dog water. After that, we call the place the "Wiener Water Tea House."

Lori and Maureen, in town to rehearse, come over to pick up Kat. My apartment is street level facing the alley, and the buzzer doesn't work, so they knock on my window to let her know they're there.

I go to First Avenue and watch them perform to a sold-out crowd. People are staring at me, so I pretend like I am really into the show. I see an edit of the "He's My Thing" meat-truck video where they cut me out and put Maureen into the shots where I once was.

Kat and I work on a few new songs together at home. She says she wants me to come back to the band, but Lori doesn't. She says she is working on that. She says she is unhappy touring all the time, feeling uncreative, like they just keep playing the same old songs. But when I see the three of them, they always seem happy together. Kat says she wants to have a new band with me and leave those two. Sometimes I believe her and keep waiting for something to happen, but always and always it never does.

Still, she can be so sweet:
She let me read her lyrics.
She let me wear her clothes.
She let me try her drugs.

But the drugs only make me sick, waking up with puke on my nightgown and a massive headache, never to be repeated again. Yet another failure: my inability to be that kind of fucked-up girl.

Kat and me,
Minneapolis, 1995

IN THE SPRING

On a winter night, after locking up the flower shop, I see an Australian Shepherd puppy in the window of the pet store down the street. She is in a little pen with a couple other Aussies, ripped up newspaper, and plastic bowls, puddles of pee. I look at her and she looks at me as the cold wind blows. I come back the next morning as soon as they open. While the other puppies go wild jumping around, she stands calmly on her hind legs and wraps her paws around my arm.

Greta runs around the Wiener Water Tea House jangling the tag with her name and my phone number on it. We go to the park; she's wrapped tightly in my coat because it's cold out, just a little brown ball of fuzz with a white stripe down the middle of her face, looking like a baby bear.

The lady next door calls the landlord because she hears Greta barking one day. There's a knock at my door. I open it and Greta runs out into the hall; the landlord can't help but smile, but also tells me I have to move out.

I see a small white house with blue trim and a white fence as I drive around one Sunday afternoon. There's a yard sign for an open house, but it's not a fancy realtor's sign—this one is written in shaky handwriting. I like it already. An old man is sitting in a recliner smoking a cigar when I go inside. He shows me around and tells me all about the place; he grew up here and planted the large black walnut tree in the front yard when he was a kid. He tells me no one wants to buy this place because the kitchen isn't updated and the wood floors are all scratched. I tell him those are not the kinds of things that bother me. He tells me, don't be afraid to make an offer, and lets me in on a secret—just how low he and his brother will go—and this amount makes for a legendary deal, payments lower than rent.

The bathroom's vintage aqua blue tiles with silver glitter, the balcony overlooking the yard. "You can open the door while you are in the tub and feel the breeze in the summertime," he tells me. There is a screened-in front porch for reading, a farmhouse-style kitchen sink. The yard is huge, and I tell him all about Greta. He tells me about the peony bushes and tulips that his mom had carefully grown.

I make wind chimes out of tarnished forks and spoons, hang them from the trees.

I make mosaics out of broken plates.

I plant my garden in spring.

THIS COULD HAPPEN TO YOU

I open my own flower store in south Minneapolis, funded on credit cards and a $3,000 loan. Greta's Flower Shop. A little place, which I paint a soft mossy green, with blooms in silver metal buckets sold by the stem and bouquets on the sidewalk when the weather is warm. Each morning I arrive with boxes of flowers in the back of the Ranchero. I call Tommy to get some advice. The manager tells me that Tommy died a few months after I left New Orleans. I don't ask how.

I do many small weddings on the weekends, but the grocery stores have just started carrying flowers, their prices the same as my wholesale costs, so it's hard to compete. In the winter, sometimes I sit there all day long, looking out the front window at the snow, reading magazines, watching the clock, only a handful of customers coming in.

One day, Tim Carr comes in and buys three wreaths, which are not my best work, spending a lot of money in my little shop. He gives them to Lori, Kat, and Maureen. In my mind, he's saying to them, "This could happen to you," but more likely he's being genuinely nice. Either way, it's embarrassing, especially when I see Lori's wreath at one of her garage sales.

The band records a couple more albums over the next few years, including a few really incredible songs; "Sweet 69" and "Right Now" are my favorites. I watch them play on MTV's *120 Minutes*. When I hear their cover of "We Are

My flower shop in Minneapolis, 1996

Family," I think about how we used to hate playing covers, that one being especially boring to me. It seems like it's been a really long time since they've had any new songs. The band's lack of inspiration is blamed on Kat's drug problems, which are growing more profound.

Lots of talk about how much the band is fighting, how severe the burnout is, the pressure from the label to sell records. How it isn't fun anymore. There are constant rumors of a breakup.

I then hear that Maureen quit because she needed hip surgery and recovery time but Lori and Kat didn't want to cancel a tour. "I told her my boyfriend would fill in, or that she could sit in a chair and play," Kat tells me. Dana, the bassist from the local band Mickey Finn, fills in for a while, but they never seem to consider her a real member.

Ignoring my instincts, I say yes when Lori calls to ask me if I want to play a show in Spain. I had just decided to start doing weddings out of my garage instead of keeping the shop open.

"I'm not playing 'We Are Family,'" I say.

HOLY WEDNESDAY

Spain is mystical and ancient, colorful and alive. We arrive a few days early so we can spend time in Granada, a town in the Andalusia region. This is where we play our first show at Espargo, the Asparagus Festival, on a bill headlined by rapper Ice-T. Lori and I wander around all day long, past street vendors selling flamenco dresses, handmade instruments, bullfight posters, flowers, and fruit. We visit the Alhambra, a fortress originally built in the year 889. Hiking up a large hill with all the other tourists, waiting in long lines, reading the plaques along the trails. We talk about how much we both have changed; there's nothing to be angry about anymore. We both acted and reacted to the best of our capabilities at the time. Now that seems so long ago. Five years: an eternity when you are young.

Kat stays in the hotel room all day and evening. She doesn't take a walk around the neighborhood to see this breathtaking Spanish town that she has never been to and may never see again. It's like we're on a family vacation and she is our troubled teenage daughter.

It is *Semana Santa*, the holy week leading up to Easter. There are nightly religious processions in Granada. On the Night of Holy Wednesday, we watch the parade, which is like a Christ-soaked Mardi Gras. It's as if we have stumbled into a Fellini movie. Dozens of men hoist ornately decorated floats and travel through the streets; cloaked barefoot figures bear huge wooden crucifixes over their shoulders;

children carry smaller crosses; actors depict the crucifixion; white-hooded men look like the Ku Klux Klan; women dressed in black hold candles; marching bands play the most somber of tunes; clouds of incense smoke rise. Floats decorated with elaborate icons and thousands of carnations pass by. People watch from their iron-railed balconies.

The whole trip is just for two shows, and we head from Granada to Vigo, a gorgeous seaside town, where we perform at another festival. Lori and I sit by the water eating platters of shrimp and spiny lobster, drinking bottles of white wine, talking to travelers who pull in by boat.

We're last on the bill, so we think we're headlining, but actually we're scheduled to play in the middle of the night. The promoter, a huge fan who is so excited to show us around town, gives us a big guarantee. By the time we go on stage, almost everyone has already gone home, and

Spain, 1997

those who remain are mostly sleeping or falling-down drunk. Before we go on stage, we feel the promoter's disappointment and can't help but take it personally. No one stayed to see us. We have mostly the same set as we did before I left the band. It feels like we are cheating, doing this the easiest way possible. The original energy and love I had for being on stage is absent. The sets take forever and even the songs I usually love do not elicit any emotion. I feel sad, empty, and lost on these big stages, knowing that while this seemed like a second chance, really it's all over.

A huge Babes fan attends both shows. He can't believe it's actually me playing, saying it's like a dream. Earlier in the day, I signed a record for him, but later when it's time to load out, he is yelling, calling out to me, wanting me to sign something else. I pretend that I don't hear him and get into our van and go back to the hotel.

The next night, I get Kat to go out. A small Spanish bar, just the two of us, many glasses empty. She won't stop crying and cannot tell me why. She isn't saying any words at all.

We sit outside on the brick steps as people walk by and stare. I promise never to leave her, the way a lover would. Knowing that Kat always survives, emerging both completely intact and blown to little pieces.

A PATH TO THE SEA

I had a dream that plays in my mind, the images scratchy and steeped in sepia: Kat and me as little girls. She is sunny and peaceful. I am talkative and squirrelly. We realize the sea is close because the air is salty and we hear the surf. We find an abandoned house built of wide-planked boards, rustic and lovely, with yellow peeling paint under a tin roof.

The house is covered in flowering vines and hidden by plumed weeds. We pull the weeds to reveal a path to the sea, cobblestone surrounded by purple thistles, vines snaking between the bricks. We head toward the water. She is quiet, calm. We follow the path and sit on the beach, sand under our feet, collecting shells and putting them in a tin can.

And then we are grown. In this dream, in the end, it is my love that saves her.

BEYOND REACH

An acquaintance from Holland sends me a DVD of Babes in Toyland being interviewed on Dutch TV, recorded shortly before I first left the band. The show is hosted by two guys who walk down a country road between segments with various bands, one drags a white bedsheet on the ground for no apparent reason, a fluffy black dog ambles behind. One of the young men looks into the camera, his face real close, announcing, "BABES IN TOYLAND!"

Lori and Kat appear on the screen standing on a small bridge over the Oudegracht, the canal that runs through Utrecht. There are old brick buildings behind them, three stories tall, apartment windows, willowy trees reflected in the water. Their names appear in block letters at the bottom of the screen. An interviewer off-camera asks them questions, struggling for the words in English:

"Was your initial plan to play really emotional music?"

"I don't think we put out a little draft like, *make emotional music*," says Kat, making motions like pen on paper. "It just comes out."

At one point, Lori looks over to where I am off-camera, and we both start laughing, only my voice present.

"It's really extreme what you do," the guy says.

"That's just the way it happened. We are really extreme women," says Lori.

"In what way?"

Lori and Kat are annoyed, fidgeting; I am still off screen.

"I mean, I just think we are three strong personalities," Lori says.

They cut to live footage: a big club, Kat in a red velvet dress, her hair flying around as she bellows into the mic. Lori wears a black tank top, jean shorts, black tights, and hoop earrings, her dreadlocks up on top of her head, the hairdo we call "the pineapple." I have on '70s flowered pants and a crochet top, a silk flower is clipped into my hair, my eyes closed as I play.

Behind my lids the sound is white light, flowing, flickering, kaleidoscopic. I am beyond reach.

Back to the canal:

"Do you think the last record was a bit of a change from the first one?"

The camera pans over to me, standing off to the side. My skin is rosy and unlined, eyes without the dark circles I always have now. A silver choker with heart charms around my neck, a necklace that I still wear. My voice high and unfamiliar, I look terrified as I speak, but look directly at the guy.

"Your style is going to evolve, not like that means bad or soft.... But you are going to change."

TALKIN' 'BOUT TOGETHER

After we released our first record, one of our favorite places to play was the Uptown Bar. We got so psyched when we sold out the place. Lori and I waited tables there a couple nights a week. The management was nice about us leaving on tour as long as we covered our shifts.

We loaded in through the back door, propped open, letting in the polar winter air. Wearing knit hats, mittens, and long johns under our dresses, Kat and I helped each other bring in the speaker cabinets, each taking one side, then assisting Lori with the rest of her drums. In the bar, people were still eating dinner, food served 'til 10 p.m., sitting in the vinyl booths, some with their kids. The cooks emerged from the basement with buckets of chopped veggies, walk-in coolers and backstage both downstairs; you passed a basket full of dirty work aprons before arriving in the hideout with table and chairs, skank couch with springs poking out, graffiti on the walls, beer on ice in a bus tub.

At soundcheck, Kat's voice caused scrunched faces and fingers in the ears of dinner guests. When we were done, we hung out downstairs and peeked up every once in a while, getting charged as the room filled. We wrote our set list on the back of an old flyer.

We would head upstairs to cash in our tickets for free rail drinks, or to watch the opening band, but mostly hung out with friends downstairs, burrowing like marsupials.

When the opening band was done, we headed out of

Kat, me, and Lori

the hovel. Leaning against the wall on stage, smoking a cigarette while tuning my bass, I thought I was badass until the smoke got in my eye, burning, tears running down my cheek, stubbing out the butt. Then two of us would look for whoever was missing, and pound one more drink for extra bravery. The packed bar buzzed like hummingbirds, full of conversations and smoke. I pushed through the dense crowd to get back to the stage, my boobs accidentally sweeping across someone's back, a random hand on my butt, just slightly, like I wouldn't notice.

The stage at the Uptown was the perfect size: we weren't too far from each other or too close. It was like a fort, snug like that. Once we started playing, the show went by in accelerated speed, a colorful streak. I wanted it to last. Seeing my favorite song coming up on the set list, my heart cracked open like an egg, so excited to play it.

Lori told corny jokes complete with punch-line rimshots while Kat or I changed a string. Kat turned her pretty head to the side and spat on the ground, then back to the mic as she announced the next song so sweetly.

After the show, we hung out upstairs and talked to the crowd, our friends lingering until the bouncers start shouting, "Time to leave... LEAVE!" Stray beer bottles everywhere, waitresses in booths counting their tips, bartenders putting away the lemons and limes, wiping up with haggard white towels, upside-down stools on tabletops. Lori sat down with the manager and laughed loudly as she collected our money.

We decided to pick up our gear the next day, when the place would feel weird, brightly lit for brunch, our equipment stowed near people's Sunday eggs. But in that moment, we just wanted to go home. The parties didn't sound fun, a few people sitting in a stale living room drinking, and the roads were slippery anyway. As we headed out the back door, the manager turned off the lights.

We got in Vanna, Lori driving, Kat in the passenger seat, me sitting on an upside-down pickle bucket in the middle. We each had a full beer hidden in our coats. We stopped at White Castle on Lake Street, getting onion chips and sliders. Lori paid out of the band money in the florescent glow, the clientele a mix of people who all seemed to have some kind of major problem. A ragged old guy asked if he could smell my hair.

Back in the van, the Guess Who song "Share the Land" played on KQ92. Lori turned it up.

Maybe I'll be there to shake your hand.
Baby, I'll be there to share the land.

When we got to a stoplight, the song went into the part repeating "shake your hand, share the land." The three of us sang "shave your hand" over and over, motioning like razors shaving the backs of our hands.

My house was the first stop. The Minneapolis neighborhoods lit by streetlight took on a blue-gray glow in the winter night, tree branches sparkled with snow like baby's breath. The impenetrable quiet.

It was cold in the van and we could see our breath as we made plans for the morning. Sitting in front of my place, Lori slipped a wad of cash into my hand, grandpa-style.

My ears were ringing, my hair stank like cigarettes, someone had spilled a drink on my dress. One of my black knee-high boots was missing a heel, I had tape on my fingers over the blisters that burst, the sliders in my belly were already starting to swell, I had drunk too much beer. So relieved to be near my bed. It was heaven to be home.

I took the key that hung on the black ribbon I wore around my neck and opened the lock of my door, aware of Vanna idling behind me. Lori and Kat waited until I was inside before they left me.

ACKNOWLEDGMENTS

I would like to thank everyone who helped bring this book into existence.

To Lori Barbero and Kat Bjelland. I am grateful for spending some of the most beautiful and important days of my life with you. I love the music we created and those nights sitting on top of the van watching the stars.

To my parents, Gloria and Arthur Leon; my brother, Harmon Leon; my sister and brother-in-law, Denise and Chuck, and the entire Venables family. For all the years. The light and heavy we've shared, for being young and older together, for the flicker of our memories, the love. You are all a part of me.

To my early readers, and everyone who helped me remember; your input was fundamental to creating this text: Sarahjane Blum, Terri Sutton, Howard Hamilton III, Laurie Lindeen, Cyn Collins, Joan Vorderbruggen, Dana Thompson, Sam Ridenour, David N. Meyer, Eva Mozey Etoll, Mike Etoll, Susan Lynn, Montana Pecore, Geoffery Trelstad, Lori Bjelland, Dawn Kuehl-Miller, Grant Young, Nicolas Destino, Pamela Johnson, and Brad Zellar.

To Mike Hopp, Jill Fonaas, Brian Garrity, JJ Gonson, Jim Conroy, Caren Faisst, Phil Harder, Glen Jones, Dave Markey, Jeroen "Buffel" Meijerink, Greg Neate, Bill Phelps, Reynard Toombs, Mark Trehus, and Gary Walker for graciously contributing photography and memorabilia.

To the friends who are always there for me: Hayley Bush, Kevin Kling, Mary Ludington, Ali Lozoff, Jeanette Bazis, Paul Pirner, Dave Paulson, and Julianne Hinchcliffe.

To the family of Joe Cole: Sally and Jerry Siebold, and Staci Bainbridge. Thank you so much for your love and unconditional acceptance. You were so generous with your time and sharing of personal keepsakes; that means everything to me.

To Katie Joan O'Brien: You are forever loved and will never be forgotten. Having your photographs grace this book makes my heart explode with both love and loss.

To Jody Statzer, my Beaver Lodge sister: here's to dancing on the couch, wearing that crusty thrift store Elvis suit, and being girlfriends. I love you, will miss you always.

To Tim Carr: You left an indelible mark on everyone. Thanks for all that you did for us. I miss your wicked smile.

To all the fans who supported Babes in Toyland by coming to our shows and buying our music and merchandise. You are exceptional, lovely, perfect. I am grateful to all of you.

To all the friends I made on the road.

To my advisors at Goddard College: Darcey Steinke, Douglas A. Martin, and Reiko Rizzuto. Thanks for helping me discover my writing voice and style.

To Shelly Mosman, for her stellar photography.

To Aimée Bissonette, for all her legal advice.

To the staff at Minnesota Historical Society Press for understanding my vision and making it real. Thanks to Pam McClanahan, Ann Regan, Dan Leary, Shannon Pennefeather, Alison Aten, and freelance copyeditor Scott Parker for all your help. To my editor, Josh Leventhal, for being calm, reassuring, and never once pressuring me about the word count.

And to my family; my husband, Steve; my children, Jae and River. You are the Fourth of July, the drive-in movies, sunshine and moonlight, ice cream sandwiches, swimming in a lake, walking in the woods. You are all the flowers. For the way you shine. For the way we drive each other crazy. For the way we work so hard and are dead tired at the end of day. To waking up holding hands intertwined unknowingly in our sleep. To living inside a pink Victorian house with a fireplace glowing all winter long and too many dogs running around. For the way we plant our garden together every single spring.

SONG LYRICS CREDITS

MOTHER

Words and Music by Kat Bjelland
Copyright © 1992 by Universal Music - Z Tunes LLC and No Dukey Music
All Rights Administered by Universal Music - Z Tunes LLC
International Copyright Secured All Rights Reserved
Reprinted by Permission of Hal Leonard Corporation

PEARL

Words and Music by Kat Bjelland, Lori Anne Barbero, and Michelle Leon
Copyright © 1991 by Universal Music - Z Tunes LLC and No Dukey Music
All Rights Administered by Universal Music - Z Tunes LLC
International Copyright Secured All Rights Reserved
Reprinted by Permission of Hal Leonard Corporation

SPUN

Words and Music by Kat Bjelland and Lori Anne Barbero
Copyright © 1992 by Universal Music - Z Tunes LLC and No Dukey Music
All Rights Administered by Universal Music - Z Tunes LLC
International Copyright Secured All Rights Reserved
Reprinted by Permission of Hal Leonard Corporation

Additional excerpts of Babes in Toyland song lyrics are by Kat Bjelland,
including "Spit to See the Shine" and "Dust Cake Boy," copyright © 1989;
and "Mad Pilot," copyright © 1991. Lyrics reprinted with permission.

PHOTO CREDITS

Unless noted below, all photos and images are from the author's collection.

Photos by JJ Gonson, pages 21 and 39.
Photos by Katie O'Brien, pages 24, 48, 50, 56, 59, 72, 82.
Photos by Jim Conroy, pages 27, 93, 108.
Photo by Phil Harder, page 36.
Photos courtesy of Jill Fonaas, pages 43 and 84.
Photos by Glen Jones, pages 51 and 52.
Photos courtesy of Eva Mozey, pages 99 and 171.
Photos courtesy of Sally Siebold and Staci Bainbridge, pages 122 and 126.
Photo by Reynard Toombs, page 131.
Poster courtesy of Greg Neate, page 138.
Photo courtesy of Lori Barbero, page 141.
Photo courtesy of Gary Walker, page 149.
Photo by Greg Neate, page 165.
Photo by David Markey, page 177.

I Live Inside has been set in Chaparral Pro—an old-style font with slab serif influences—which was created by Adobe type designer Carol Twombly in 1997.

Book design and composition by
Ryan Scheife at Mayfly Design, Minneapolis, MN.